To Bolton Bridge

Yew Close B.

Tythe Barn Close

Church

Bailey

Walk

Cowmans Croft

Mr Shaw

Clithero School

Henry Alcock Esq

1. Craven Bank
Birch & Thompson

Dring Close

Metcalfe

Vicarage

Tythe Barn Close

RCH STREET

Red Lion

Thanet Arms

Chancery Lane

Mr Bradshaw

National Schools

Lane

Rope Walk

The Currer Flats

Old George

o School

Clithero School Land

CLITHERO SCHOOL LAND

Back

Currer Croft

Bank

Lane

Late Revd T Gartham

Skipton School

Gram School

Main

Wilson Esq

Mr Back

Back

Carr

Mr Preston

Mr Durr

Brown Esq

Independent Chapel

Miss Leuning

R Smith

To Rumbold's Moor

Esqr

NEWMARKET

Tradesmen's Place

James Park

Cha. Carr. Esqr

John Dyneley Esqr

Mr Ross

Smith Esq

T Wood Heelis Esq

Grant

Old House

Cha. Carr. Esqr

Esq

Mr Smith

Beck

Cockhill

Population in 1821 8,411.

1 2 3 4 5 6 7 8 9 10
Scale of Chains

A B Rawson

The Book of Skipton 1983
has been published as a Limited
Edition of which this is

Number   378

A complete list of the original
subscribers is printed at the
back of the book

To Richard from Dad

13.4.1983

R. Geoffrey Rowley

THE BOOK OF SKIPTON

FRONT COVER: Horse Fair, Skipton c1920.(Drawing by Kenneth Holmes)

Parish Church and Skipton Castle grounds, 1982. (DH)

THE BOOK OF SKIPTON

BY

R. GEOFFREY ROWLEY LLD

BARRACUDA BOOKS LIMITED
BUCKINGHAM, ENGLAND
MCMLXXXIII

PUBLISHED BY BARRACUDA BOOKS LIMITED
BUCKINGHAM, ENGLAND
AND PRINTED BY
HOLYWELL PRESS LIMITED
ENGLAND

BOUND BY
J W BRAITHWAITE & SON LIMITED
WOLVERHAMPTON, ENGLAND

JACKET PRINTED BY
CHENEY & SONS LIMITED
BANBURY, OXON

LITHOGRAPHY BY
BICESTER PHOTOLITHO LIMITED
BICESTER, ENGLAND

DISPLAY SET IN BASKERVILLE
AND TEXT SET IN 11/12pt BASKERVILLE BY
HARPER PHOTOTYPESETTERS LIMITED
NORTHAMPTON, ENGLAND

© Geoffrey Rowley 1983

ISBN 0 86023 177 1

Contents

Acknowledgements

My thanks are due to the staff of Skipton Public Library, Keighley Library, Bradford Central Library (Local Studies), Leeds City Library, Yorkshire Archaeological Society, and to the members of the Skipton and District Local History Society — established by Mr George Hunt, and flourishing.

The Craven Museum was opened in 1928, and in 1936 it was taken over by Skipton UDC. It has since been transferred to more spacious premises adjoining the Town Hall, with the generous help of Mrs J.B. Coulthurst OBE and the Coulthurst Trust. I am grateful for the museum's help and the cooperation of the Craven District Council.

I have made use particularly of W.H. Dawson and of Dr Whitaker, though the latter's work is largely a history of stately homes and county families; I would have been lost without the three volumes of the Skipton Parish Registers, edited by W.J.Stavert.

Thanks are also due to all the people who have contributed photographs for copying. One of them I mention by name — I have to express my thanks to Ken Ellwood, not only for pictures, but also for information as to who has been depicted, and for his practical assistance and enthusiasm throughout the gestation of this book, and Frank Knowles of Leeds.

I acknowledge also the help, among others, given by the firms of Hepper Watson and Dacre Son and Hartley and of the *Craven Herald* which first suggested the project, without whom, and the subscribers who have supported me, this book could not have been published in this form.

I am a native of Skipton. Both my grandfathers married and died in Skipton. My father served on the Skipton Urban District Council from 1943 to 1961 and was Chairman in 1950-51 and again in 1959-60. So I share the love of Skipton which has been bred in me.

Finally, this work could never have been undertaken without the active participation of my wife Valentine, and for her interest and help I shall ever be grateful.

Bibliography

Ackernley, M. (Sub nom Arty Momus) *Ticklers* (1882)

Clay, Sir Charles *The Honour of Skipton* (1947)

Clifford, A. *Collectanea Cliffordiana* (1817) (reprint 1980)

Dawson, W.H. *History of Skipton* (1882); *History of Independency in Skipton* (1891); *Loose Leaves of Craven History* 1 ser. (1891); *Loose Leaves of Craven History* 2 ser. (1906)

Dixon, J.H. *Chronicles and Stories of the Craven Dales* (1881)

Ellwood, J.K. *Skipton, A Pictorial Recollection* (1975); *Life in Old Skipton — A Photographic Recollection* (1982)

Foster, J. *Elementary Education in 19th Century Skipton* (1976)

Gibbon, A.M. *The Ancient Free Grammar School of Skipton in Craven* (1947); *100 Years old. The Story of the Skipton Mechanics' Institute* (1947)

Holmes, M. *Proud Northern Lady* (1975)

House, Mrs J.S. *The History of Scouting in Craven* (1907-1965)

Raistrick, A. & S.E. *Skipton — A Study in Site Value* (1930)

Ranger, W. *Report to the General Board of Health — Skipton* (1857)

Renn, D.F. *An Angevin gatehouse at Skipton Castle* (1975)

Rowley, R.G. *Old Skipton* (1969)

Stavert, W.J. *The Parish Register of Skipton in Craven*. 1592-1680 (1894), 1680-1771 (1895), 1745-1812 (1896)

Ward, J. *Skipton Castle 2 Edn.* (1877)

Waterhouse. R.R. *Skipton R.D.C. 1894-1974 A Short History* (1974)

Whitaker, T.D. *History of Craven*, 3rd Edn. (1878)

Williams, D. *Mediaeval Skipton* (1981)

Williamson, G.C. *Lady Anne Clifford* (1922)

Foreword

by Councillor Bernard O'Neill, Skipton Town Mayor

History is a peculiar thing. It can be a dry, dusty, chronology of dates, prominent personalities, and momentous happenings in the past. On the other hand it can be presented as a moving, living, tapestry of the life and times of our ancestors and predecessors.

How it is presented is utterly dependent on the skill and expertise of the historian and, as this book bears witness, we have been extremely fortunate in having as our recorder Dr Geoffrey Rowley LLD.

To his undoubted scholastic skill, he has added a depth of research and understanding of his subject matter, that far surpasses anything I have previously read about the history of Skipton.

When additionally the author has such a great depth of feeling for the town and for the community, both past and present, then the reader too becomes engrossed in the rich fabric of the history as it was lived, and can almost become contemporary with the people and the events which have eventually provided the Skipton we love and enjoy so well in present times.

I am confident that this book will, in due course, become required reading for all those who wish to know and understand the major influence Skipton had in the formation of Craven.

Bernard O'Neill

Preface

by N.D. Simpson, Chairman of Craven District Council

Skipton is my town. I was born in Skipton and brought up in the district. I have spent all my life and made my living in or near the town; and it is therefore an honour and a delight to have been asked to provide a preface to Dr Rowley's book.

Geoffrey Rowley, as a practising solicitor, has accumulated a vast knowledge of the history of the town. Its people, its buildings and its character come alive in his book. His interest in the subject is obvious and his affection for the place is apparent.

Skipton is a fascinating town. It is truly the gateway to the Yorkshire Dales, and is the centre for an extensive rural hinterland. Although the character of the place may have changed over the years there are few Skiptonians who would wish it to be any different from what it is — a small, homely, country market town in which everyone who lives in the area, and many from further afield, take a deep personal interest.

Most visitors, whether sightseeing or shopping, come to Skipton because they have made a conscious decision to do so and not because the town is *en route* to somewhere else. They recognise a town which has changed with the times but has managed to retain its character and attractions.

I am glad that Dr Rowley has written this book. He is well known as a local historian and his knowledge of the town can now be shared by a wider audience. 'That is a good book which is opened with expectation, and closed with profit'. (Alcott)

N.D. Simpson

ABOVE: An 1830 view of the Parish Church and Castle; BELOW:
Middle Row, c1850.

Introduction

There is a widening interest shown in the history of our own neighbourhood. In this book, I have tried to illustrate local events in the context of the national past, but it is still not a history book.

For history has not come to a full stop; it just feels like that. The 19th century tailed off, leaving a number of questions unresolved, such as what is to be done about the redeveloping of the central area — Albert Street and Victoria Street — whose old houses were demolished in 1956.

What, if any, are the market rights for stallholders? A learned case in 1961 brought forth the following exchange: asked by Mr Athorn about market days, Mr Robinson said that the matter was not straightforward. Commented Judge Withers Payne: 'Nothing in Skipton ever is'.

Perhaps the floods in 1979 and 1982 suggest a freak rainfall, or perhaps atmospheric changes worldwide. What impact will be made on shopkeepers by the northern by-pass, and by the imposition of parking fees in the Town Hall car park? The problems of the present leave us limp with foreboding.

The area is well served by its historians. Dawson's old (1882) *History of Skipton,* his occasional articles issued in two series of *Loose leaves of Craven History,* and a *History of Independency,* which paid tribute to his own family and faith, all comprise the basic material for the study of the town's past — a classic instance of a local writer who cannot be surpassed.

Yet 'One of the multifarious duties which we owe to posterity [is that] we must place in the front rank that which prompts us to chronicle for the special edification and guidance, anything and everything which may be the remotest chance be either interesting or instructive.'

If *The Book of Skipton* is both interesting and instructive, then it will have been worth the writing.

Dedication

To my wife and family

ABOVE: J. Tasker dedicated this 1830 view of the (upper) High Street to Charles, Earl of Thanet. It was engraved by J. Scarlett Davis; CENTRE: a slightly later etching of the same period shows more of High Street (referred to by Wood in his 1832 map erroneously as Church Street); BELOW: the 7th century gold French *tremissis* found in Skipton. (DH)

In the First Place

Skipton lies at the junction of several valleys in the lowlands just to the north of the Aire river, in the shadow of the millstone grit hills of three moors, on a gravel bed formed by glacial action.

From time to time early man occupied hill sites around the later town site, during the Mesolithic and Iron Age periods, but earlier Neolithic man passed this way, leaving flint flakes and a boring tool behind, in what was later Canal Yard, and a small cup in Keighley Road. Yet the town almost certainly has an Anglo-Saxon origin, probably dating to the settlement following the AD 615 Battle of Chester.

The site may have been chosen for defensive purposes, but is more probably the product of available water, good drainage, pasturage and woodland. A natural route junction, Skipton profited from early tracks and possibly the Roman route from York to Elslack — Roman coins have been found in abundance near today's Newmarket Street.

By Domesday, Skipton was still only a tiny settlement within a major, originally Saxon estate, and even possibly unoccupied, while certainly in a state of neglect. The de Romilles created the first castle, and this laid the seeds for the future town's prosperity and significance.

Skipton bears an Anglo-Saxon name (*sceap* — sheep, and *tun* — town) which later adapted to a Norse pronunciation. The regular Anglo-Saxon pronunciation is witnessed in the name of Shipley.

There are no written records of Skipton earlier than Domesday (1081-86), but the earlier date for the settlement is suggested by the discovery in 1978 in the church-yard during construction work, of a *tremissis* — a French gold coin of the 7th century.

The Domesday entry reads as follows:
'Manor. In Bolton Earl Edwin had six carucates of land to be taxed.
Berwick. In Halton 6 car, In Embsay 3 car, inland and 3 car. Soke. Berwick. In Draughton 3 car, Skibeden 3 car, Skipton 4 car, Snaygill 6 car, Thorlby 10 car.
Soke. Beamsly 2 car, Holme 3 car.'

All this holding is surveyed under the head of *Terra Regis,* on account of the forfeiture of Earl Edwin's possessions. Shortly after Domesday these estates formed the major part of the land granted to Robert de Romille. Edwin was Earl of Mercia and his estates devolved on his great-nephew William de Meschines, who married Cicely, the daughter and heiress of Robert de Romille.

The ancient parish of Skipton comprised the townships of Skipton, Embsay-with-Eastby, Barden, Beamsley, Bolton Abbey, Draughton, Halton East with Bolton, Hazelwood-with-Storiths and Stirton with Thorlby.

13

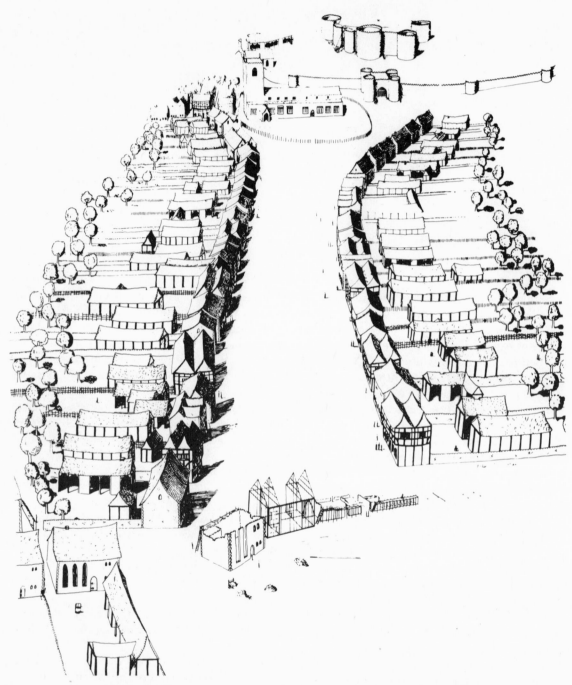

Mediaeval Skipton — a reconstruction by Peter M. Williams. (DW/CDC)

The Cliffords

The Cliffords took their name from a village near Hay, on the Welsh border. In about 1273, Roger de Clifford married Isabel, one of the two co-heiresses of Robert de Veteripont. The Veteripoints had been granted the Barony of Appleby, or Westmorland, with the Castles of Appleby, Brough, Brougham and Pendragon.

Robert de Clifford, according to Sir Matthew Hale in his *Memoirs of the Cliffords,* was from his infancy 'educated in the school of War, under King Edward I, as good a master, for valour and prudence, as the world afforded. In 1297 the King appointed him Governor of Carlisle, to repress the insolence of the Scots, which he did with much civility and courage'. The King summoned him to Parliament as one of the peers of the realm, and granted him estates in Scotland.

Robert de Clifford was doubtful whether he could hold the Scottish land from a base in Herefordshire and, in March 1310, he obtained the Honour of Skipton, castle and land to the value of £200 per annum, half for life and half in tail (ie with a revision on the extinction of the line, to the donor — the Crown). In August 1310 he exchanged lands in Monmouthshire for an enlarged grant of the whole of the Honour in tail, and in September 1310 the King released the excess over £200, granting the Honour 'as fully as the Earls of Albermarle held the same.' Robert was slain at the battle of Bannockburn in 1314.

Notes on the Clifford family show that the terms 'Lord of Skipton,' and 'Lord of the Honour of Skipton', are used indiscriminately. The second lord is (in Whitaker) referred to 'Roger Lord Clifford, Second Lord of the Honour of Skipton'. This could create problems, as there is no relation between a peerage and an Honour; a peerage is a dignity conferred by the Crown; the Lordship of an Honour is an interest in real property. For our purposes, it is assumed that Robert was the first 'Lord of Skipton', received a peerage by summons to Parliament in 1300 and on the occasion of a number of later Parliaments, and that numbering of the Lords Clifford (whether with or without the superfluous 'de') should date from 1300.

Times now became tumultuous, between the King and the barons . . . Hale records: 'A number of northern nobles entered into a confederacy under the Earl of Lancaster, on the pretence of effecting necessary reforms. King Edward II defeated the barons at Boroughbridge. Three days later a military Court was held at Pontefract, where the King in person, with loyal peers, pronounced judgment of death against the rebels, including Roger, and all his lands were seized into the King's hands, as forfeited.'

Roger 2nd Lord Clifford (1299-1322) has been variously reported as having been executed at York, and as having been respited by reason of his great wounds. He died in 1322.

In the Parliament of 1330-1 there was a general act of restitution of all who were in the company of the Earl of Lancaster, and all their lands restored. Hale wrote: Robert 3rd Lord Clifford (1305-1344) 'rose with the rising sun, King Edward III, by which means he had the opportunity to recover the inheritance which his elder brother's misfortunes, and the troubles of those times, had for a while lost. He was a favourite of both the Edwards. He prudently matched his young son in his lifetime to a family in power in the north, and died after he had lived Lord of Skipton in possession 28 years.'

Robert 4th Lord Clifford (1330-1350) was only 13 years of age at his father's death, and in ward to the King, he married Euphemia, daughter of Ralph Lord Neville of Middleham. Of Roger 5th Lord Clifford (1333-1389) Sir Matthew Hale continues, 'much cannot be said of this Roger because there is little upon record or in history concerning him.' He retained Sir Robert Mowbray, for peace and war, at ten pounds per annum salary for it was the practice of nobles at that time to retain persons of valour in their employment.

There was great distress in the country following the Black Death (1348-50), followed by the Statute of Labourers (1351), which forbade workmen from demanding more than they were wont to receive before the plague. To raise money, Richard II introduced a Poll Tax in 1377, again levied in 1378. When the tax was repeated in 1380, it aroused the wrath of the peasantry, and led to the 'Peasants' Revolt,' and there were riots as far north as Bury and Beverley, but there is no record of any revolt in Skipton.

However, the Lay Subsidy Roll for Staincliffe in 1379 illustrates life in Craven at that time. All inhabitants over 16 years of age are listed, except the clergy, who were taxed separately, and mendicants, and the rolls indicate which taxpayers were married. Skipton, the seat of the Honour of Skipton, was rated at 35s — less than Marton — but this is due to the fact that neither the Cliffords nor any of their principal officers were in residence in Skipton Castle when the tax was levied, although they had held the Honour since 1310, and Roger de Clifford was at this time 5th Lord of the Honour. As a baron his tax would have been 40s.

Skipton was a thriving clothing centre, with four weavers, two fullers, five tailors, a draper, a glover and a cobbler. Catering was the province of a 'harbeiour' (lodging-house keeper, probably an inn-keeper), a butcher and two spicers. A merchant, roper, mason, smith and lorimer made up the business community. The herbergour was Rayner de Silsden, who paid 12 pence, and may well have been the landlord of what is now the Red Lion Inn.

In Skipton there were three 'websters', Peter Brabaner (from Brabant), his son, and William Webster. Indeed, 12 out of the 33 weavers in Staincliffe are named 'webstre', 17 out of the 38 tailors are 'Taillour' and just over half of the blacksmiths are called 'smyth'. At this time hereditary surnames were not fully developed, and the Poll Tax Assessments may have hastened the adoption of second descriptive names. Apart from their occupations, tax-payers are identified by their place of origin, and the Skipton list features Stephen de Malham, Robert de Leeds, Thomas de Wrose and Peter de Thorpe. The third mode of description was the family name, as in William Rogerson or 'Adam filius Elie' (Ellison). Family descriptions are not confined to sons and Grassington records the delightful Isabel Snekdoghter.

Thomas 6th Lord Clifford (1364-1391) was a favourite of King Richard II, and just as extravagant and degenerate. It is said that, two years before he entered upon his father's domains, he was charged by the Parliament with having aided the King in his dissolute conduct.

Holinshead writes that in about 1390 'William Douglas of Nidderdale was chosen by the lords of Prutzen to be admiral of a navy containing 240 ships, which they had rigged, and purposed to set forth against the miscreant people of those north-east parts. But being appealed to by the Lord Clifford (an Englishman who was then likewise to serve with the foresaid lords in their journey) to fight with him in a singular combat. Before the day came appointed for them to make trial of the battle, the Lord Clifford lay in wait for the Douglas and upon the bridge of Danske met with him and there slew him, to the great disturbance and stay of the whole journey'. This Lord Clifford was slain in Germany in 1391. He had held the Honour for only two years.

Of John 7th Lord Clifford (1389-1422), Hale says 'John's mother negotiated a treaty of marriage with Elizabeth, only daughter of Henry Percy, son of the Earl of Northumberland, this was solemnised when John was not much above 15 years of age'.

In 1415 he accompanied Henry V in an expedition to France. Two years later he seems to have been retained by the King for the French wars. In recognition of his faithful conduct and signal service, he was elected a Knight of the Order of the Garter; he was killed at the siege of Meaux, in 1422, when only 33 years of age, and was buried at Bolton Priory.

A Compotus for 1437 shows that the gross receipts from the Honour of Skipton were £269 0s 8d and the net receipts only £113 6s 8d. Thomas 8th Lord Clifford (1415-55) was present at the siege of Pontoise in 1439. The unpopular King Charles of France attempted to recover the town, which Thomas had surprised by strategem and bribery. Charles came with ten or twelve thousand men; Lord Clifford's strategem was to array his men in white, the ground being covered with snow, and so approach the fortress unobserved.

Thomas supported the Lancastrian party at the outbreak of the Wars of the Roses; he was killed at the Battle of St Albans in 1455, and was interred with his uncle Henry Percy, Earl of Northumberland.

Dr Whitaker's account of John 9th Lord Clifford (1430-61), 'Black-faced Clifford' is succinct: 'partly from the heat of youth, and partly in the spirit of revenge for his father's death, [he] pursued the House of York with a rancour that made him odious, even in that ferocious age. His supposed slaughter of the young Earl of Rutland in, or perhaps after, the battle of Wakefield, has left a deep stain upon his memory; and his own untimely end, which happened the next year, is remembered without regret. On the day before the Battle of Towton and after the *rencontre* at Ferrybridge, having put off his gorget, he was struck in the throat by a headless arrow, out of a bush, and immediately expired'.

He was attainted in 1461-2, and the castle, manor and lordship of Skipton were granted in tail male to Sir William Stanley. In 1467-8 there is a deed of resumption and in 1475-6 the estates were granted to Richard, Duke of Gloucester, and were held by him until his death. In 1485-6 the attainder of John Lord Clifford was reversed, and the estates of the family restored to Henry his son.

On the accession of Henry VII, Henry 10th Lord Clifford (1453-1523) emerged from the fells of Cumberland, where he had been principally concealed for 25 years, with the manners and education of a shepherd. He was at this time almost, if not altogether, illiterate, but far from deficient in natural understanding and what strongly marks an ingenious mind in a state of recent elevation, depressed by a consciousness of his own deficiencies. On this account he retired to the solitude of Barden, where he seems to have enlarged the tower out of a common keeper's lodge, where he found a retreat equally favourable to taste, to instruction and to devotion. The narrow limits of his residence show that he had learned to despise the pomp of greatness, and that a small train of servants could suffice him who had lived to the age of 30, a servant himself.

Wordsworth wrote:

'Our Clifford was a happy youth,
And thankful through a weary time,
That brought him up to manhoods prime.
Again he wanders forth at will,
And tends a flock from hill to hill:
His garb was humble; ne'er was seen
Such garb with such a noble mien.'

He was interested in the motions of the heavenly bodies, and in alchemy. Whitaker cannot resist a comment: 'This much, however, may be said in favour of alchemy, that, however subservient to fraud or superstition, it was never, like modern chemistry, degraded into the handmaid of atheism'.

In 1485 Richard III was slain at the Battle of Bosworth, and his successor Henry VII, married Elizabeth, daughter of Edward IV in 1486. Henry Clifford came out of hiding and petitioned for the restitution of his estates. In 1513, when almost 60 years old, he was appointed to a principal command in the army which fought at Flodden.

In Lady Anne's Memoirs he is described as 'a plain man, who lived for the most part a country life, and came seldom either to Court or London, excepting when called to Parliament, on which occasion he behaved himself like a wise and good English nobleman'. He died in 1523, aged about 70.

There could scarcely have been more difference between the 10th Lord, brought up on the fells as a shepherd, and his son Henry the 11th Lord who had been educated with King Henry VIII. The father had complained bitterly to the Privy Council about his son's behaviour — disobeying his commands, threatening his servants, and stealing his goods; when he came into the country he apparelled himself and his horse in cloth of gold 'more like a duke than a poor baron's son that he is'.

The King was not unappreciative of his friend and in 1526 created him Earl of Cumberland (1493-1542). His household accounts record 'My Lord's expense riding to London' as 'First paid for my Lord's expense, and 33 his servants, riding from Skipton to London, as appeareth by the household book £7 15s 1d'.

In 1533 the new Earl was created a Knight of the Garter.

In 1536 Earl Henry remained loyal to the Crown during the Pilgrimage of Grace, when all other northern strongholds had surrendered. Robert Aske led the rebels, who required Henry to join them; his reply was to assure the King that, although 500 gentlemen retained at his own cost, had forsaken him and joined the rebels, yet he would continue the King's true subject and defend his Castle, in which he had great ordnance, against them all.

It was said that 40,000 rustics assembled in Yorkshire, furnished with 'Horse, Armour, Artillery and habiliments of war threatened to set the stay of Estate upon the props of their giddy inventions'. Their pretence was religion, and defence of holy church; so forward and fervent were they in their proceedings that this attempt must be termed a Holy Pilgrimage.

The demands of the rebels were (i) the restoration of the religious houses; (ii) remission of the recently made subsidy; (iii) exemption of the clergy from payment of tithes to the Crown; (iv) repeal of the Statute of Uses; (v) the removal of villein blood from the Privy Council; and the deposition and punishment of the heretic Bishops Cranmer, Latimer, Hilsey, Brown and Longlands.

Skipton Castle ultimately surrendered to the rebels, but shortly after, the rebellion was quashed, Aske was executed at York, and his body hanged in chains.

A short time before his death, as a reward for his courage and loyalty, Henry received a grant of the Priory of Bolton, with all the lands in the parish of Skipton thereto belonging, together with the manors of Storiths, Haselwood, Embsay, Eastby, Cononley, etc, and the Manor of Woodhouse (part of Appletreewick).

At the age of 16 years, Henry 2nd Earl of Cumberland (1517-70) was made a Knight of the Bath at the coronation of Queen Anne Boleyn, and by the King's interest in 1537 he married Lady Eleanor Brandon, daughter of Charles Brandon, Duke of Suffolk, by Mary Queen Dowager of France, daughter of King Henry VII.

The eastern part of the Castle terminating in the Octagon Tower was built by the first Earl in 1536 for the reception of Lady Eleanor. She died in 1547, and was buried at Skipton. Her husband was so much affected that, on hearing he was a widower, he swooned, and fell into a languishing sickness, being rendered to such an extreme state of weakness that his physician thought him dead. His body was already stripped, laid out upon a table, and covered with a horse-cloth of black velvet, when some of his attendants perceived symptoms of returning life. He was once more put to bed, and recovered, but for a month or so his only sustenance was milk suckled from a woman's breasts, which restored him completely to health.

His Royal wedding had necessitated large expenditure, and he was compelled to sell the manor of Temedbury in Herefordshire but, after Lady Eleanor's death, he withdrew into the country, grew rich, and became a purchaser. He had a good library, was studious in all manner of learning, and much given to alchemy.

At the age of 18, George 3rd Earl of Cumberland (1558-1605) married Margaret, daughter of Francis Earl of Bedford, by whom he had two sons, both of whom predeceased him, and one daughter, the Lady Anne Clifford.

He is remembered best as a licensed buccaneer, and as such his expeditions were expensive and not productive. They all took place between 1586 and 1596. The Queen supported her loyal subject but, instead of the financial assistance he hoped for, in 1587 the Queen included him in the list of 40 peers who were commissioned to try Mary Queen of Scots and, after her attainder, he was one of the four earls who was sent down to Fotheringay Castle, to be present at the execution. In 1592 he was rewarded with the Order of the Garter. At an audience with the Queen after one of his cruises, she dropped one of her gloves, which he took up and presented to her on his knees. She desired him to keep it for her sake, and he adorned it richly with diamonds, and wore it ever after in front of his hat at public ceremonies. When the Queen's Champion, Sir Henry Lea, resigned, Elizabeth appointed George to be her own peculiar champion at all tournaments.

To the right of the archway in the Gate-house of Skipton Castle, is the 'Shell House' — so called because one of the lower rooms in the apartment was decorated with sea shells, fixed in cement. Over the fireplace Neptune is shown. The shells are said by tradition to have been brought by the third Earl from one of his expeditions.

Whitaker sums up this Earl as a 'great but unamiable man. His story admirably illustrates the difference between greatness and contentment, between fame and virtue. If we trace him in the public history of his times, we see nothing but the accomplished courtier, the intrepid commander, the disinterested patriot. If we follow him into his family, we are instantly struck with the indifferent and unfaithful husband, the negligent and thoughtless parent. If we enter his muniment room, we are surrounded by memorials of prodigality, mortgages and sales, inquietude, and approaching want. He set out with a larger estate than any of his ancestors, and in little more than 20 years he made it one of the least. Fortunately for his family, a constitution originally vigorous gave way, at 47, to hardships anxiety and wounds. His separation from his virtuous lady was occasioned by a court intrigue; but there are families in Craven who are said to derive their origin from the low amours of the 3rd Earl of Cumberland'.

The Parish Register records his death: '1605, October 29, departed this life George Earl of Cumberland, Lord Clifford, Vipont and Vescy, Lord of the Honour of Skipton in Craven, Knight of the most noble order of the Garter, one of his highness privy counsel, lord warden of the City of Carlisle and the Welsh Marches, and was honourably buried at Skipton, the 29 of December, and his funeral was solemnised the 13th day of March then following'.

His bowels and inner parts were buried in the Chapel of the Savoy. He died of the bloody dysentery caused, as was supposed, by the many wounds and distempers he received formerly in his sea voyages. Shortly before he died he laid the seeds of future litigation.

Francis the 4th Earl (1559-1640) was born in Skipton Castle in 1559 and died in the same apartment more than 80 years later. Lady Anne observed of him, that he and his estate were governed by his son Henry Clifford for the last 20 years of his life. Whitaker acidly wrote that Lady Anne 'had an excellent hand at drawing characters; but the best painter of the face, or of the mind, is confounded by absolute vacuity'. His wife died in 1613, and after her death Earl Francis resided almost always at Skipton.

Earl Francis was succeeded by Henry, the 5th and last Earl of Cumberland (1591-1643). Lady Anne seems to have borne him no animosity, for she wrote that he 'was endued with a good natural wit, was a tall and proper man, a good courtier, a brave horseman, an excellent huntsman, and had good skill in architecture and mathematics'.

He died 'of a burning fever' and was buried in Skipton Church in December 1643. His eldest daughter, Elizabeth, married Richard Boyle, Viscount Dungarvan, eldest son of the first Earl of Cork in 1634, in the chapel within Skipton Castle.

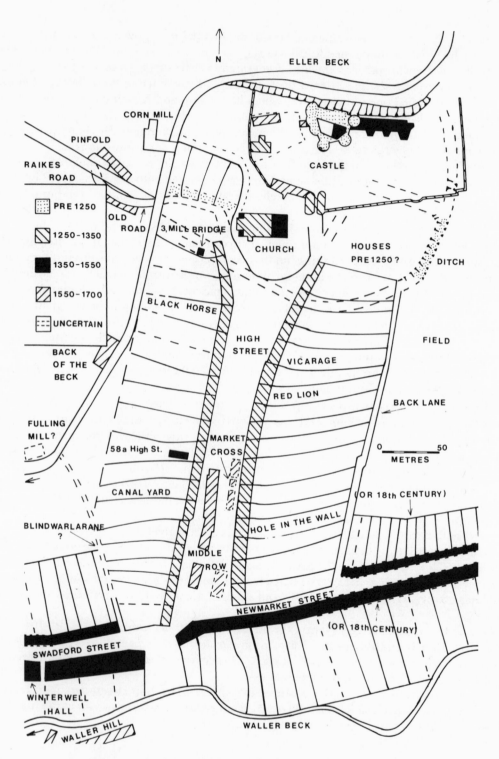

The growth of the town between c650 and 1700. (DW/CDC)

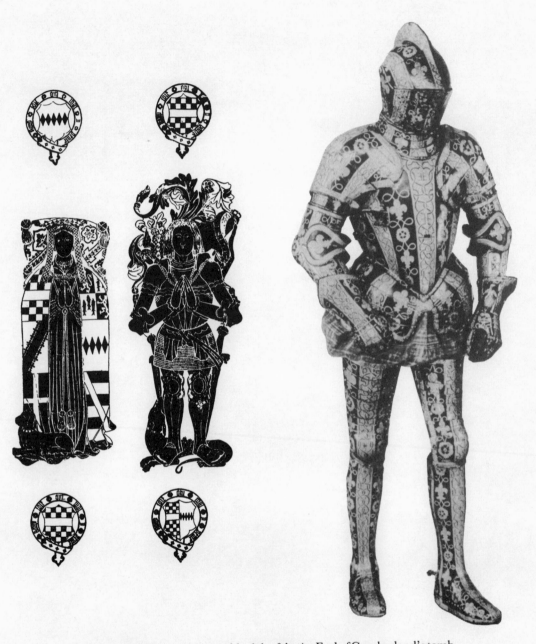

LEFT: Buttresses on the marble slab of the 1st Earl of Cumberland's tomb in the Parish Church, (JW) and RIGHT: the 3rd Earl's armour — now in the States.

George, third Earl of Cumberland (1558-1605). (SCL)

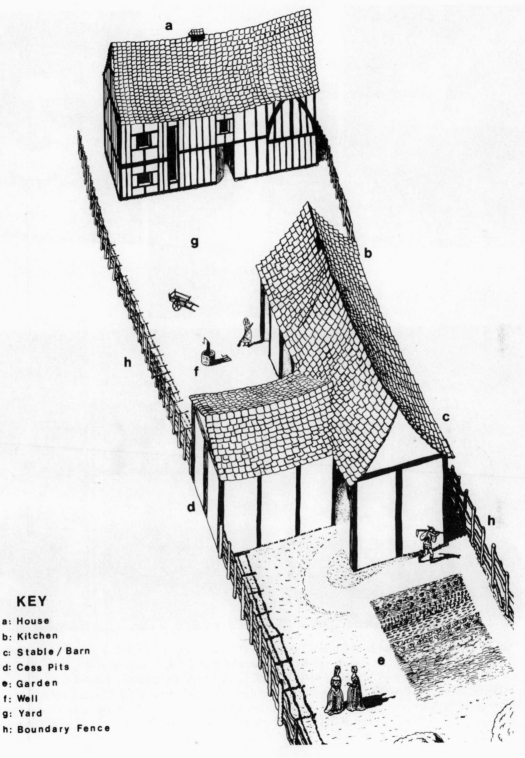

KEY

a: House
b: Kitchen
c: Stable / Barn
d: Cess Pits
e: Garden
f: Well
g: Yard
h: Boundary Fence

Canal Yard c1450. (DW/CDC)

23

ABOVE LEFT: Lady Margaret Russell, Countess of Cumberland (1560-1616) and Lady Anne's mother; (SCL) CENTRE: Thomas Tufton, 6th Earl of Thanet (1644-1729) — known as the 'Good Earl; (SCL) and RIGHT: Lady Anne Clifford (1590-1676); (SCL) BELOW: the triptych, housed at Appleby Castle; (AHAG) CENTRE PANEL: George, Earl of Cumberland, Lady Anne Clifford's father, Lady Margaret his wife, Lady Anne's mother and their sons, Francis and Robert; LEFT: Lady Anne Clifford aged 15 yrs; RIGHT: Lady Anne Clifford aged 56 yrs.

Castle and Kin

After the death of Henry 2nd Earl of Cumberland, Dr Whitaker continues 'From this period I shall, in great measure, make the Cliffords their own biographers; and shall extract the materials of their history from the celebrated family portrait (the Triptych) the long inscription on which was drawn up by Lady Anne Clifford, Countess of Pembroke, assisted, according to tradition, by the celebrated Sir Matthew Hale'. The Triptych was painted by George Perfect Harding (d1853). There were originally two copies, one at Appleby and the other at Skipton. The Skipton copy was sent to Hothfield. The other copy is in the Great Hall at Appleby Castle.

Lady Anne's passion for detail knows no limit. Who else except Lady Anne, would record for posterity that she was a daughter and sole heir of 'George Clifford, 3rd Earl, by his worthy wife Margaret Russell, Countess of Cumberland, of whom her mother conseyved with child in Channell Row in Westminster the 1st day of May 1589 and was delivered of her the 30th day of January following in Skipton Castle in Craven'?

The central panel of this painting shows George the 3rd Earl with the Countess Lady Anne, and their two sons Francis and Robert. The right-hand picture represents Lady Anne in a black gown edged with lace, with a double row of pearls for necklace and also a pearl girdle. Her hair is brown and long, with long ringlets at each side of her head. The left-hand picture shows Lady Anne at the age of 15.

Lady Anne Clifford (1590-1675) was born at Skipton Castle on 30 January 1590. At the age of five she was seriously ill, and given up for dead, and in her childhood narrowly escaped death by water and fire; at the age of 19 she married Richard Sackville, Earl of Dorset. They had two daughters — Margaret (born 1614) and Isabel.

In 1607 Lady Anne and her mother came from London to Appleby, and also stayed briefly at her castles in Brougham, Brough and Pendragon. On 22 October 1607 they came to the gates of Skipton Castle, but were denied entrance, by reason of the suits of law between them and Earl Francis.

She was left a widow in 1624, and six years later she took a second husband, Philip Herbert, Earl of Pembroke and Montgomery.

Lord Dorset was not a faithful husband. He had children by Lady Venetia Stanley, whom Lady Anne is reported to have brought up under her own care. There was also a notorious woman of the town called Bess Broughton. Yet Lady Anne spoke of him in affectionate terms: 'This first lord of mine was in his nature of a just mind, of a sweet disposition, and very valiant in his own person'. Of her second lord she is also indulgent: 'He was of a very quick apprehension, a sharp understanding, very crafty withal, and of a discerning spirit . . . He was one of the greatest noblemen of his time in England, in all respects and was throughout the realm very well beloved'. A less glowing description was that of 'an ingrate, an ignoramus, a common swearer, a bully and a coward'.

When James II had arrogated to himself the office of arbitrator, all parties agreed that they would accept his award — except Lady Anne. She had already been warned by the Queen not to trust the King lest he should deceive her. Dorset knew that he had everything to gain — in ready money — and little to lose, if the award was upheld. But he did not like the King's manners, and could not help admiring the way Lady Anne stood up to them.

Lord Pembroke died in January 1649-50, and thereafter she resided alone wholly on her northern domains. She moved regularly from castle to castle and 'diffused plenty and happiness around her, by consuming on the spot the produce of her vast domains in hospitality and charity'. Wherever she was staying, every Monday morning she caused 10s to be distributed among 20 poor householders of the place, beside the daily alms she gave at her gate to all that came.

She restored her castles, and repaired the churches. But she followed an obsolete mediaeval model, so leaving the estates encumbered not by one, but by five inconvenient structures, which were expensive to maintain, and not required as residences by the Lords of the Honour.

She also built Almshouses at Appleby, in the spirit of the Beamsley almshouses built by her mother.

To what extent the re-building of useless mediaeval memorials is charitable may be doubted. Is the work of any folly-builder charitable because it provides work? It was claimed that this extended programme was itself a benefaction to the people of Westmorland, because it provided employment for countless workmen 'by which she did set the poor on work, as well as supplying their indigency'.

Dr Whitaker sums up: 'She was one of the most illustrious women of her own or of any age . . . She was the oldest but most independent courtier in the Kingdom; had known and admired Queen Elizabeth, had refused what she deemed an iniquitious award of King James: re-built her dismantled castles in defiance of Cromwell'. Dawson says 'Lady Anne Clifford has left an example of noble living which will be an honour to womanhood for all time'.

Most commentators have related the stories of the parliamentary candidate and of the boon hens.

Sedgwick (Lady Anne's Steward) writes that there had been paid for 400 years continuous to the Castle of Skipton 800 boon hens yearly, and the like to the Castle of Appleby. One Murgatroyd, a rich clothier of Halifax, who had bought a tenement, was to pay one hen. This he flatly refused to do, so Lady Anne brought an action against him at York Assizes, and recovered the value of the hen, though it cost her £200, and Mr Murgatroyd as much. The story of her inviting Mr Murgatroyd to dine, and having the hen served up between them, has no contemporary authority.

During the 'great law-suit', a corrupt minister of Charles II attempted to force her to return a ministerial member for one of her own boroughs, contrary to her own sentiments. She retorted: 'I have been dictated to by a King. I have been bullied by a usurper, but I will not submit to a subject. Your man shall not stand'. This reply attributed to her by Horace Walpole in 1753 has long been discredited as an 18th century fabrication.

The prolonged disputes as to the inheritance of the family estates can only be understood in the light of English real property law. An estate granted to a donee 'and his heirs' passed the entire interest in the property, which was known as the 'fee simple.' A grant to be a donee 'and the heirs of his body' created a 'fee tail', that is, an estate which would last as long as there were lineal descendents of the donee in existence; if this line died out, the estate reverted to the original grantor or remainderman. The entail could be barred, but not where the remainderman was the King.

The grant could be limited so as to subsist only as long as there were heirs male of the body of the original grantee; this was known as a fee tail male. The Earldom of Cumberland had been granted to Henry, the first Earl and the heirs male of his body, so it expired on the death of Henry, the 5th Earl. The titles of baronage and the lands granted in 1310 descended to Lady Anne. By his will Henry the 2nd Earl purported to bar the entail; George the 3rd Earl died likewise, but both of them overlooked the fact that they could not bar the entail as long as the reversion remained in the Crown.

On the death of Earl George, his widow Lady Margaret claimed the entailed estates for her daughter, Lady Anne. The reply by Earl Francis was that Parliament had authorised the grant; that the confirmation by Richard II amounted to a new grant of the fee simple; that by the Act of Attainder 1461 and Act of Restitution 1485 it was turned into a fee simple and that it was settled as a freehold by Earl George. Francis then took alarm and obtained a grant to himself and his heirs of the reversion, so that the reversion would no longer be vested in the King.

In 1310 the Honour of Skipton was granted to Robert de Clifford in tail; this entail could not be barred — and thereby converted into a fee simple — as the King was entitled in remainder. It passed down in the family until the death of George the 3rd Earl, when the Earldom of Cumberland went to Francis the 4th Earl.

In 1617 the King took upon himself the awarding of this difference, and ordered that a conveyance of the said Honour be made by Lady Anne (then Countess of Dorset) and the Earl her husband, to Francis Earl of Cumberland for life, remainder to his first and other sons in tail, remainder to the Countess for life, remainder to his first and other sons, remainder to her daughters, and £20,000 was to be paid by the Earl of Cumberland to the Earl of Dorset.

To this award the two Earls subscribed, but notwithstanding the potency of the Earl of Cumberland, the will of the King, and the importunity of a husband, the Countess refused to subscribe or submit to it.

On the death of Henry, the 5th Earl, in 1643, the estates passed to Lady Anne, and the law-suit settled itself. She travelled round her northern domains, scattering monumental inscriptions behind. Perhaps the most famous of these was 'the Countess Pillar' erected to commemorate the spot where she last saw her mother, on the roadside near Brougham Castle.

From Lady Anne's death in 1675, to 1849, the Honour of Skipton was held by nine successive Earls of Thanet. This unexpected acquisition by the Tufton family had surprisingly little impact on the Castle or the town of Skipton. Their principal seat was at Hothfield, in Kent, and they now inherited the Westmoreland Estate of the Cliffords, with a seat at Appleby.

Lady Anne died at Appleby and her estates devolved on the sons of her daughter, Lady Margaret Sackville. Lady Margaret had married John Tufton, second Earl of Thanet, in 1629; she was then 14 years of age and he was 20. Lady Anne notes in her diary, that on this date 'had I the happiness to see my eldest daughter married to John Lord Tufton'.

The first Lord Tufton was ennobled in 1626. It appears that this gentleman, then a Baronet, held a patent for life in the Green Wax Office in the Kings Bench. The King, Charles I, was anxious that this should be surrendered to him, and it appears that Nicholas stipulated for an earldom: this was granted by Royal warrant in 1628.

Lady Anne left her estates to her only surviving daughter, Lady Thanet, during her life, with successive remainders to her grandsons John, Richard, Thomas and Sackville in tail, with remainder to her eldest grandson Nicholas in tail, 'not for any want of affection or goodwill in my thoughts, but because he is now by the death of his father, possessed of a great inheritance in the southern parts'. This is surprising; Lady Anne was fully aware of the difficulties of breaking an entail, and it is curious to find that by her father's will and by her own will, she provided the setting for another family dispute. On her death in 1675, Nicholas, the third Earl, took possession of the whole estate, and claimed that he was entitled under an earlier entail. Litigation was avoided by the death of Nicholas without issue in 1679.

When Nicholas was summoned to attend the King in France in February 1638, he offered a doctor's certificate and £1,000 for the performance of his services. In 1642 he joined the King at York, but returned hence 'very infirm'.

Nicholas had been a liberal contributor to Royalist funds. When he returned to England in 1655, after a long period of travel abroad, he was committed to the Tower on a charge of conspiracy against the Protector. He was released in 1658. The family compounded with the Parliamentary Commissioners during the rebellion, for the enormous sum of £9,000.

John, the fourth Earl (1638-80) was only Lord of the Honour for a few months. The Skipton Parish Register contains the entry: '27 April 1680, the right honourable John Earl of Thanet died at Skipton Castle, and his corpse was embalmed and carried away from hence to be buried at Rainham in Kent on 12 May in the vault there amongst his ancestors'.

His successor was Richard, the fifth Earl (1640-1684), who held the title and estates for only four years. *The Leeds Mercury* reports that on 27 December 1682 he ran a foot race for 100 guineas cash in St James's Park with the Duke of Grafton. Their Majesties were among the spectators. The Duke won by at least a quarter of a mile. Richard is said to have died with a barren reputation for generosity from his law-driven and impoverished tenants. Unmarried, on his death the estates passed to Thomas, the sixth Earl.

Thomas (1644-1729), and his tutor George Sedgwick, secretary to Lady Anne, had a pass to go beyond the seas in 1656, and spend the winter at Utrecht. In 1658 he had a pass to go in to the Spaw with his sister Frances, and he was at Blois with his brothers Richard and Thomas in 1662.

In 1668 he refused to stand for Appleby as Lady Anne's nominee, being 'in favour of country life'. He was one of the Tory peers who signed a protest against the Act of Union with Scotland in 1707.

His third daughter, Margaret, was married to John, Earl of Clare, son of the second Duke of Newcastle. As no moneys seemed to be coming Thomas's way, he tried to prove that the Duke must have been mad. In 1692 he fought a duel with his son-in-law in Lincolns Inn Fields. He claimed that he had his sword against Lord Clare's breast, but generously would not thrust home. In Mackay's *Chronicles* he is described as a 'thin, tall, black, red faced man of 60 years old; he is a good country gentleman, a great asserter of the prerogatives of the monarch and the church'.

Whitaker dignifies this Earl as 'a nobleman of the old school' and writes that he held the Honour of Skipton and applied the revenues of it, better than any of his ancestors, with the exception of Anne Clifford, whose spirit seemed to revive in him; he was a true son of the Church of England, virtuous, decent and charitable. He is said to have appropriated £1,500 per annum to charities, and was known as the 'Good Earl'. Swift claims that he gave away £60,000 in his life and at his death left £40,000 to trustees to distribute to different charities.

The estates now devolved on his nephew Sackville, the seventh Earl (1688-1853), Sackville the eighth Earl (1733-1786), and Sackville the ninth Earl (1769-1825).

The ninth Earl spent much of his early life abroad. In a letter in 1791, William Wyndham reports that Thanet had arrived in Paris 'with a Hungarian lady whom as a brilliant achievement he carried off from her husband at Vienna'. He married the lady, Anne Charlotte Bojanowitz in 1811 at St George's, Hanover Square, having, it is said, previously married the lady when abroad.

On his return to England he engaged desultorily in politics, in opposition to Pitt. When Arthur O'Connor was tried in 1798, Thanet and others were charged with having created a riot in Court, and with putting out the lights in an attempt to rescue the prisoner. Sheridan represented the Earl, who was found guilty and sentenced to six month's imprisonment in the Tower, and a fine of £1,000 and bound over for seven years on security of £20,000.

In 1808 the Castle was put in repair for the reception of Sackville, ninth Earl, who attended the fortnightly fair, and expressed much pleasure at the flourishing state of this northern cattle mart. In October of the following year 'Skipton Castle is now fitting up in an appropriate style the celebration of the intended Jubilee on 26th'. The Earl appears to have paid a short visit to Skipton every year, using it as a 'staging post' on his journeys to Appleby.

The ninth Earl died without issue at Chalons, where in his later years he mostly resided. He died of a complication of disorders — mortification in the legs, erisipelas, cholera morbus, fever and gout. He was a great gambler and is stated to have won £40,000 in one night, breaking the bank twice, and to have lost £120,000 another night at the Salon des Etrangeres in Paris.

He was succeeded by his brother Charles (1770-1832) the tenth Earl, who appears to have continued the brief visits to Skipton.

Henry, the eleventh Earl (1775-1849) was the last Earl, and the Earldom of Thanet became extinct when Henry died unmarried in 1849. He left his estates to his natural son by a French lady, Richard Tufton, born in Verdun in 1813, and who was naturalised in 1849, and created a baronet in 1851. He married Adelaide Amelia Lacour in 1843. Sir Richard's son was Henry James Tufton, born in Paris, who was elevated to the peerage as Baron Hothfield in 1881. He was a Lord in Waiting to Queen Victoria in 1886 and was known as an agriculturist and horse-breaker, and as a collector of miniatures.

By his will in 1848 Henry, the last Earl of Thanet left his estates to Richard Tufton for life; with remainder to Richard's issue in tail. This was subject to three conditions, first, that the beneficiaries should adopt the name and arms of Tufton; secondly that any alien beneficiary was naturalised; and thirdly, that any beneficiary who was a member of the Roman Catholic Church renounced that faith.

Henry James Tufton fought four unsuccessful elections — East Kent three times, and Westmorland once. He received his peerage from Gladstone, but became a Unionist in about 1890, and in 1895 rated as a Conservative.

In 1883 he was possessed of 17,093 acres in Westmorland, 11,953 acres in the West Riding of Yorkshire, and 10,144 in Kent and 86 acres in Cumberland, a total of 39,276 acres worth £45,937 a year.

The Tufton family have left little to remind the people of Skipton of their associations with the town. A public house was known as the Thanet's Arms Inn (this is now Scene Interiors), at the rear of which was Thanet's Arms Yard; Thanets Place is now Cross Street, and Tufton Street is part of Keighley Road. Sackville Street gives access to Middletown. The Hothfield family is recalled by Hothfield House and Hothfield Terrace and, since trustees managed the estates, two of them being George Dawson and Rowland Bennett, we have in Middletown, George Street, Dawson Street and Rowland Street, and (in Newtown) Bennett Street.

The first Lord Hothfield died on 29 October 1926 at his London residence, 2 Chesterfield Gardens, at the age of 82 years. He was born in Paris on 4 June 1844, and both father and son were naturalised by a special Act of Parliament in 1849. Skipton Castle was one of his seats, though for a good many years he had not used it as a residence, except for short periods. When the late King Edward VII was Prince of Wales, Lord Hothfield was one of his intimate friends.

For his last 24 years Lord Hothfield had been a prominent member of the Conservative party, although for 40 years before this he was liberal. The break occured in 1893.

The Honour of Skipton was held under the Hothfield family settlements and by their family estate companies, Veteripont Estates Limited and Veteripont Limited (named after Isabella de Veteripont, the mother of the first Lord Clifford) until 1959.

Skipton Castle played a part in the Second World War, when it was used by the British Museum for material from its Department of Manuscripts (now part of the British Library) 1941-1946.

In an article *The Museum in War Time,* Sir John Forsdyke (Director and Principal Librarian of the British Museum 1936-50), conceded that the Castle afforded no better protection against bombs than country houses 'but it is in a district which was strangely free from air raids'.

There were objections to using the Castle as a repository; the ground floor rooms were too damp, none of the upper rooms could be used without underpinning. Nevertheless the two larger upper rooms, the Banquetting Hall and the Toddy Room, were underpinned, and heating and racks installed, providing safe accommodation for large numbers of manuscripts, with writing facilities.

The Minutes of the Museum Trustees on the subject are concerned mainly with storage conditions in the Castle, and give little information on what was actually stored there. The British Library, whose officers have been most helpful and painstaking, say that a passing reference suggests that the papers of Sir Robert Peel, the 19th century Prime Minister, were stored at Skipton.

About 1,600 boxes of reference books and manuscripts were returned to London in January 1946.

The Skipton estate was sold in 1956, when the land found ready purchasers, but not the Castle. No one — not even the Council — would 'buy expense' as they called it. The Castle was rescued by a well-known local family who formed a small private company, Skipton Castle Limited to keep alive the memories of the illustrious Cliffords. Preservation work on the Castle has been maintained, and continuous efforts have been made to attract sufficient visitors to make the costs of preservation at all supportable.

ABOVE: Skipton Brass Band in front of the Gatehouse entrance to Castle, with the Clifford motto DESORMAIS (Henceforth), over the entrance; (SCL) LEFT: Conduit Court, Skipton Castle and RIGHT: the Clifford Shield in the Conduit Court.

LEFT: Lady Anne's entrance, Skipton Castle; (SCL) RIGHT: Maj Gen John Lambert (1619-1683), sometimes called 'Cromwell's Understudy' — he slighted the Castle (as little as possible) and was a native of nearby Calton; (SCL) BELOW; Thanet's Arms, early 1900s.

ABOVE: Tudor wing and octagonal tower of the Castle, built by the 1st Earl of Cumberland; (SCL) CENTRE: the Territorials receive their colours at the Castle, early this century and BELOW: the walls dwarf an Edwardian assemblage.

My Free Chapel

To the west of the Castle lie the remains of the Castle Chapel, of which several of the windows and the original doors are distinguishable, and also the piscina. The chapel was used as a stable for many years, but its remaining original features are now on display.

In 1314-15 Robert de Clifford was possessed of the Castle 'with the free chapel of St John the Evangelist'; and Whitaker refers to a confirmation by Henry Lord Clifford in 1512:
'Know ye me to have seen certain evidences belonging to my Free Chapel of John Evang within the Castle of the foundation of the Earl of Albermarle, presently belonging to me, in which are contained certain liberties and duties to the Parson, or Chaplain, and his successors; and also one copy of certain of the same evidences are written in two mess books, one new, and the other old; in one of which the said Earl granteth that the said Chaplain shall have meat and drink sufficient within the hall of the Lord of the Castle, for him and one garcon with him. And if the Lord be [absent], and no house kept, then he and his successors shall have for every ten weeks one quarter of wheat, or 6s 8d and 4s in money.'

An inquisition in 1323 found that Alice de Romille (1155-87) granted that the Chaplain celebrating in the chapel of the Castle and his successors should receive every 12 weeks a quarter of wheat, and yearly at Christmas 13s 4d for a robe. The Earls of Albermarle followed Alice de Romille as Lords.

A return of 1284-5 shows that of the 10 carucates (a carucate — between 60-80 acres of ploughland) held in honourial demense in Stirton-with-Thorlby, a carucate had been assigned for the celebration of masses in the chapel of Skipton Castle.

In 1576 a warrant names 'Sir Will Stubbs', parson of my Castle of Skipton'. In 1542 Sir William Thirkeld was presented to the living, and was still the incumbent, then 48 years old, when chantries and free chapels were dissolved in 1548, and Thirkeld was granted 100s for life. In 1552, on the grounds that there were doubts as to whether this was a free chapel or a parsonage, an order from the Augmentation Office allowed Thirkeld to remain in possession of the parsonage (and its income) for the time being.

Whitaker continues: 'When this incumbent died or what became of him, I do not know, but upon his demise or removal a scheme seems to have been formed by the Clifford family to present no more chaplains, and to suffer the endowment gradually to sink into oblivion: for in 1572-3 a commission was granted to Richard Assheton and John Braddyll, the purchasers of Whalley Abbey, to institute an enquiry *de terris concelatis capellae de Skipton',* in consequence of which the old endowment once more came to light, and the chapel with its appurtenances was sold to Francis Procter and Thomas Browne'.

In 1573-4 these partners assigned the premises once more to a John Procter who, in 1575-6 conveyed the whole to George Earl of Cumberland.

A valuation of 1612 returns: 'The Free Chapel and lands belonging, then extended at 86s 8d was, by inquisition, found concealed upon the statute of chantries, and came to the King's hands, and the late Earl purchased them again — NIL!'

In July 1634 Richard Viscount Dungarvon married Lady Elizabeth Clifford in the chapel, and their daughter Katherine was baptised in the chapel in October 1637. There is a brief reference

Richard Waller's 1840 view of his native High Street, before the market
cross went.

to the marriage in the household books, to the effect that the clergyman officiating was 'Mr Francis Clever BA of Divinity, chaplain in house with the Earl of Cumberland and the Lord Clifford, unto whom God send a thousand million of joys'.

Whitaker, writing in 1805, notes: 'The sacred edifice is now a stable. In whose time, or by whose order, it was perverted to that indecent and disgraceful use I do not know, but it may be affirmed without risk though without evidence, that it retained its original destination till after the death of Thomas the Good Earl of Thanet'. (1729)

It was through the 1635 marriage of Lord Dungarvan with Lady Elizabeth Clifford — daughter of Henry the fifth Earl of Cumberland, that a part of the Clifford Estates passed to Viscount Dungarvon — eldest son of the first Earl of Cork, in which family they continued for four generations but, on the death of Richard, third Earl of Burlington, they fell to the family of Cavendish, by the marriage of the Earl's daughter Charlotte, with William fourth Duke of Devonshire.

34

Pulpit and Parson

The finding of the *tremissis* perhaps from a burial suggests there may have been a church in early Saxon Skipton, but the first mention of such a building is in the late 1120s — the church of Holy Trinity — probably a wooden structure. It was assessed at £30 in 1291 and by 1326 was probably a masonry structure. It was certainly rebuilt in stone by the 14th century. It was enlarged in the following century, and badly damaged in the 17th. It was restored in the 19th century.

Not until 1342 did it become the practice for Bolton Priory to present Canons to its vicarages, and the first recorded Vicars of Skipton were lay clerks. This explains how Stephen of Bradley, who was presented in 1267, came to be rejected by the Archbishop of York on the ground of his illiteracy.

The Endowment of the living is dated 16 September 1326, when Henry de Erdeslaw (Ardsley-upon-Dearne) was Vicar, and mentions the 'mansion in the town of Skipton, which the Vicar used to inhabit'.

In 1342 Bolton Priory appointed one of its Canons, Thomas de Manningham, to the vicarage; probably being past work he was turned out to grass. He was one of the eight canons who were billeted out in 1320, on account of the poverty of the Priory — due to the Scottish incursions and to its debts; in 1322 Archbishop Melton had to send Thomas back from St Oswald's to Bolton, as his enforced hosts at St Oswald's were suffering 'unbearable famine, sufficient to stab and pierce with its sharpness the bowels of ourself and of every worshipper of Christ'. In November 1350 Archbishop Zouche ordered an enquiry into complaints about the conduct of 'brother Thomas of Manningham, sometime a canon regular and professed in the monastery of Bolton, who acts as vicar of the parish church of Skipton'. The accusations are not specified, but Thomas resigned the Vicarage in 1354.

In the next century a vicar, Richard of Wintringham, met an unfortunate end. On Sunday 11 October 1401 John, son of Sir William de Rylestone, and others lay in ambush between Sawley Abbey and Gisburn for the vicar; John wounded him in the back with a barbed arrow, so that he died two days later. John was indicted for murder in the King's bench, but later pardoned.

Gilbert Marsden was suspended by Archbishop Rotherham from the office of Prior of Bolton in 1481, for loading the house with debt, and for 'vain and immodest amours with suspect women'. He resigned shortly afterwards, and was presented to the Vicarage of Skipton in 1490; he resigned in 1512.

William Blackburn became the first Protestant Vicar of Skipton in 1521. In 1534 he was presented to the Rectory of Marton. Froude has written that Robert Aske, the leader of the uprising known as the Pilgrimage of Grace, (1536) with 40 of their retainers, made their way to Skipton Castle. A day after their arrival the Earl's whole retinue rode off in a body to the rebels. Unfortunately Lady Eleanor Clifford, her three children, and several other ladies were staying at Bolton Abbey at this time. The insurgents threatened that, on the day following, Lady Eleanor and her party would be held as hostages for the Earl's submission, and if the first attack failed they would 'violate all the ladies and enforce them with knaves under the walls'.

In the dead of night the Vicar, William Blackburn, Christopher Ashe, a groom and a boy stole through the insurgents' camp, and crossed the moors with led horses, by unfrequented paths, and reached the safety of the Castle. As Lady Eleanor Brandon did not marry Lord Henry Clifford until 1537, this must be regarded as romantic fiction.

When William Ermysted founded Skipton Grammar School in 1548, he named Thomas Jolly as Vicar of Skipton.

Prior Moone had surrendered Bolton Priory in January 1538-9. The advowson was on 31 August 1542 granted to the Dean and Chapter of Christ Church, Oxford.

Richard Gibson was installed in 1587; in 1581 he had been instituted to the Vicarage of Gisburn, which he vacated in favour of Skipton. In 1591 he exchanged the living of Skipton for the rectory of Marton. He died in 1631.

Robert Sutton was Vicar from 1621 to 1665; his son Thomas (baptised at Skipton in 1640) succeeded his father as Vicar until 1688, and was also Vicar of Carleton (also held by Christ Church, Oxford) from 1674. The Reverend Oliver Heywood in his diary comments on the son in 1681. 'He is a strange man — he will drink till three or four o'clock on Sabbath morning, yet preach and rant it about drunkenness, notably in the pulpit. He saith himself that he had the knack of preaching. Oh, dreadful!'. The Parish Register entry of his burial reads, 'the best of preachers and a very peacable good man'. One can only reflect upon the words of Dr Johnson: 'In lapidary inscriptions a man is not upon oath'. The Sutton family remained in Skipton, and the Earl of Thanet's pensioners at Christmas 1710 includes a payment 'To the three daughters of Mr Sutton, former Vicar of Skipton, one of them bed-rid another very helpless all very poor — £5'.

Timothy Farrand, Minister at Bolton since 1680, was Vicar from 1683-85. He was also Master of Skipton Grammar School from 1674 to 1685. His wife was a niece of William and Sylvester Petyt.

George Holroyd MA, Vicar from 1685, was living at the Vicarage at the time of the Poll Tax 1698. He resigned the living in 1705, and died in 1712-13.

Roger Mitton, the son of Roger Mitton, a Starbotton blacksmith, graduated at Jesus College, Cambridge, in 1686 and was ordained a priest in 1689. He became Vicar of Kildwick from 1697-1705, and Vicar of Skipton until his death in 1740.

Jeremiah Harrison MA, was a pluralist vicar: he held Long Preston from 1730 to 1763, and also served at Skipton from 1740-48. His daughter, born at Long Preston vicarage, recalled that her father was 'twice a year plentifully supplied with venison by the noble owner of Skipton Castle from the park at Skipton'. Harrison was also a JP and Vicar of Catterick.

Walter Priest MA, (1748-69) was a resident vicar, the first of the Christ Church, Oxford graduates to hold the living. He married Catherine, daughter of Richard Barrow, a Skipton chandler. A Terrier of 1764 describes the church property: 'One slated Dwelling House on the east side of the town of Skipton near the Church in length 37ft the breadth unequal built with stone containing five rooms on the ground floor (to wit) the entrance from the street into the Hall 12ft and a half foot long and six foot wide with a stone floor and ceiled One Room called the Hall 18ft square with stone floor and ceiled One parlour 15ft long and 11 ½ ft wide and floored with deal hung with paper and ceiled One closet 11ft and a half long six ft wide stone floored and ceiled One kitchen 18ft long and 11ft broad stone floored One milkhouse 11ft and a half long and six ft wide stone floored and ceiled under the Hall One cellar 11ft and seven inches long and nine ft and five inches wide stone floored and arched made by the present Vicar. The five upper rooms much of the same size two of which upper rooms are hung with paper and ceiled another of the said Rooms ceiled the other two Rooms not ceiled. Also adjoining to the above there is a slated house and shop next the street built with stone in length 31ft and ½ feet and in breadth 11ft and a half stone floored one Chamber ceiled the others not. Contiguous to this and under the same roof is one thatched barn with a stable in length 34ft and in breadth 23ft. Also contiguous thereto is one Garden fenced with a stone wall of 96 yards in length and 23 yards in breadth. All bounded on South East by property occupied by John Wellock and on North by property occupied by Abraham Dixon'.

36

During Mr Priest's incumbency disputes arose about the liability to tithes which were settled by the freeholders of Skipton conveying to Walter Priest a plot of common land on Rombalds Moor in satisfaction for tithe hay and tithe herbage in the parish. The Deed was confirmed in 1757 and Mr Priest died in 1758. Dawson records that immediately after this Deed the land was let to a wealthy inhabitant at a fabulous rental. Time passed on, and the lease expired; with its expiration the value of the land sank to its natural level, and the vicar received only a sixth or a seventh of the sum at which the land was first let. 'That the whole business was a bit of clever cunning if not to use a stronger word — there can be no doubt. The living was as a consequence very materially impoverished. It was probably from this reason that the two vicars preceding Rev P.C. Kidd held the living of Kildwick in addition to that of Skipton'.

David Poate MA, from Hampshire, was a Merton graduate and held office for two years only, from 1769 to 1771.

John Parry MA (1771-78), a Welshman, was 27 when he came to Skipton, having graduated at Christ Church. To put it mildly, he was odd. An advertisement appears in the *Leeds Mercury* in June 1776:
'A curate to do the Constant Duty of the Parish Church of Skipton is immediately required. Constant residence will be expected, 40 guineas per annum'. In the same year the churchwardens' accounts record a payment of 12s 11d, 'for seeking the Vicar when lost'. The parish register in 1778 refers to 'the Reverend John Parry Vicar (but insain)'.

In January 1776 the creditors of John Parry gave notice 'that they had become possessed [under an assignment thereof to them made by the Clerk of the Peace of the West Riding] of the Benefice and Estate and Effects of the said John Parry'; a fund was to accrue from the Benefice after a deduction of £52 10s to be annually paid out, by the direction of the Ordinary of the Diocese to provide a proper person for doing the Duty of the Church. Creditors were asked to lodge claims with Mr Alcock, Solicitor.

Richard Hind MA, DD was Rector of Shering, Herts in 1754, Rector of Bishop Stortford in 1754, of St Annes, Soho in 1766, Prebendary of St Pauls in 1773, and Vicar of Rochdale from 1778. He never resided at Skipton, and Richard Withnell was his resident Curate at Skipton from 1774 to 1794; Richard Hind died in 1790 aged 75.

Thomas Marsden MA (1790-1806) was resident Vicar of Kildwick, and he retained Withnell as his curate, and tried to get him appointed to the Mastership of the Grammar School in 1792. Mr Marsden's son, Dr William Marsden, was a physician at Ship Corner, Skipton until 1868.

John Pering MA (1806-43) continued the 65 years during which Skipton was without a resident incumbent. *The Leeds Mercury* of 29 August 1818 reports: 'The congregation assembling for public worship at Kildwick Church in Craven experienced a severe shock last Sunday, from the Vicar, the Rev Mr Pering, having been seized with a fit in the middle of the sermon, which laid him prostrate in the pulpit. We are happy to add the reverend gentleman was speedily restored, by the means of some timely application, and enabled to finish his sermon, to which the image of death, as exhibited in the countenance of the preacher during his indisposition, imparted a moral stronger than any language could convey'.

Pering was a University College graduate; he was a wealthy bachelor who drove a carriage and pair. His memorial in Kildwick Church recites: 'In his estimable character all those qualities were combined which distinguish a man and elevate a Christian in whom learning was adorned by humility, benevolence by modesty and piety, by a life of self-devotion to his God'.

In August 1843 Philip Chabert Kidd was inducted to the Vicarage. He was born in 1818, and was one of the four sons of the Rev Thomas Kidd all of whom became clergymen. Educated at Norwich Grammar School and Christ Church, Oxford, he was reputed to be the best Greek scholar in the Deanery. He married Sarah, the eldest daughter of Henry Alcock.

The 1326 Endowment of the Vicarage provided that the Vicar should bear the ordinary and accustomed burdens, except the rebuilding and reparation of the chancels, 'which the Religious shall do when necessary', but extraordinary expenses shall be discharged by the Religious and the Vicar for the time being according to their portions. At the dissolution of Bolton Priory, the Dean and Chapter of Christ Church, Oxford, became, and still are, the impropriators of the living of Skipton.

The church was struck by lightning in a severe thunderstorm, during divine service on 19 June 1853. The west pinnacle of the tower, weighing a ton and a half, fell. There was panic among the congregation.

J.A. Cory, of Durham, was the architect appointed to report upon the needful repairs, and he reported that several beams of the roof of the nave had been rendered insecure by the shock, 'the pillars beneath the east gallery are evidently in a bad state, and the arches should be properly shored up, and all the five pillars effectively under-pinned'. The estimated cost was £1,470, of which Christ Church contributed £620. Not all the recommended alterations had been rendered necessary by the storm. It has been suggested that the Oxford College was becoming concerned at the liability for repairs appurtenant to the 'great' or rectorial tithes, and in 1867 they ceded these tithes to the Vicar in order to augment the endowment, the benefice becoming a rectory. The Rev P.C. Kidd had moved to the present Rectory in 1861.

On 13 April 1925 the organ was struck by lightning, and partially destroyed. There is an eerie story that a large crowd had gathered in the church-yard and the adjoining streets; those near the church heard the weird strains from the damaged organ, which played its own funeral dirge as the hot air rushed through the pipes.

In the Parish of Skipton in 1831 there were 6,200 inhabitants, of whom the eastern part of the parish were provided with church accommodation at Bolton Abbey. This left 5,000 to the superintendence of the Vicar. The parish church would only accommodate 900 in pews and 250 children on benches and steps. If half the inhabitants were at all times able to attend church, there would be a deficiency of accommodation for 1,500 persons. Under these circumstances Christopher Sidgwick, whose pride and joy this project was, proposed the building of another church.

In 1836 an agreement was made with Christ Church, Oxford, patrons of the living of Skipton, that the patronage of the new church should be with the Vicar of Skipton.

On 21 June 1837 the foundation stone of the new church was laid — the first in Craven for 300 years.

The *Christ Church Magazine* of 1887 relates the following story: The stone laying had been fixed for Wednesday 21 June 1837 and when the day arrived it was known although not generally, that the King (William IV) had died the previous day. Part of the programme was that God Save The King should be sung, but doubts were expressed as to the propriety of it under the circumstances; however, sung it was, the word 'King' being taken to mean reigning monarch, according to the French proverb: 'The King is dead, long live the King!'. The ceremony was a simple one, the clergy assembled at the Black Horse and moved to the site where a service was begun by Mr Pering, the Vicar of Skipton.

In 1843 Christ Church, Oxford gave land and buildings, being the old tithe barn in Swadford Street. The parsonage was built in 1845-6.

Daniel Parsons MA was the first incumbent of the living. His reputation had not gone before him. The *Leeds Mercury* of 8 February 1840 reported as follows: 'The Rev Daniel Parsons, the Puseyite curate of the New Church, Skipton has left that town, his doctrines being so unpalatable that he had a very scanty congregation. He preached his last sermon, the previous Sunday and resigned the living'.

Richard Ward was appointed in June 1840. He was curate of Leeds, an office he resigned in 1845. He presented a small silver flagon for use at Holy Communion at the reopening of St Stephen's Catholic Church, Skipton. Another beautiful sermon was preached by Ward, who had formerly been a protestant clergyman in this very town in which he was proclaiming the truth of the Catholic faith. Many of his former flock, to whom he had been much endeared by his charity to the poor, his zeal and unaffected piety, earnestly listened to their former minister, while he enforced the duty of inquiring into the grounds of their faith.

There followed John Blair, MA, Curate of New Shoreham 1846-9, Wright Willett, 1849-1862, and William Henry Clarke, 1862-1883, incumbent of Herringfleet, near Lowestoft.

In 1884 a new brass lectern was presented to the church by the family of Christopher Sidgwick, one of the founders of Christ Church.

In 1885 there was also unveiled a stained glass window on the south side to the memory of the late Dr MacNab. The remaining vicars were: G. A. Blair, 1883-99; R. Thorman, 1899-1920; G. E. Alvis, 1920-1927; C. R. Chappell, 1927-44; R. H. Place, 1944; H. A. Atkinson, 1953; M. B. Slaughter, 1963; and D. A. Carpenter, 1976.

ABOVE: Tasker's 1857 engraving of the Parish Church and BELOW:
'curious openings' found in the 1909 restoration.

ABOVE: Parish Church plate; CENTRE: Skipton Parish Church 1909; LEFT: the then Archdeacon Cook inspecting the new bells in August 1921, and RIGHT: west gallery in Parish Church, removed 1909.

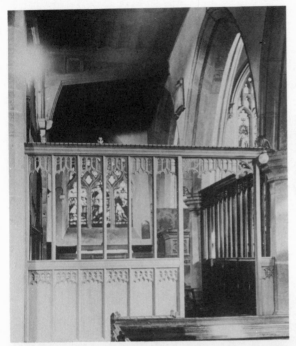

LEFT: New Parish Church screen designed and carved by H.C. Foster;
BELOW: Christ Church, built 1837-9, and RIGHT: the interior.

LEFT: View of High Street from Church c1900; BELOW: from the church tower c1930, and RIGHT; Christ Church Vicarage, now a block of shops known as Central Buildings; OPPOSITE ABOVE: the 'bus station in Caroline Square in the 1920's, and BELOW: Skipton Show, 1870.

43

ABOVE: The cattle market in High Street c1900, and BELOW: the market at the top end of the High Street. Middle Row is in the background. The raised path led from the stone setts above the Town Hall to the Church and can still be seen today.

44

ABOVE: In 1897 the Council commemorated the Diamond Jubilee of Queen Victoria by planting trees in High Street; one is seen here lying on the Setts; BELOW: a view up towards the Church, c1940.

ABOVE LEFT: The Wheatsheaf Inn closed in 1913; RIGHT: a bit of old Skipton, 1897; BELOW LEFT: Chancery Lane off High Street now part of Rackhams; RIGHT: the Market Cross and stocks in High Street before 1840.

46

ABOVE LEFT: Four old cottages stood near to the Cross with diamond
leaded windows; RIGHT: the Town Hall before the canopy was removed,
and BELOW: today.

ABOVE: Sheep Street before 1914; CENTRE LEFT: the Kings Arms before demolition, and RIGHT: partially demolished; BELOW LEFT: the empty site, and RIGHT: replaced by Silvio's and the Gift Shop.

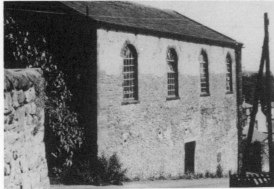

ABOVE LEFT: The New Ship Inn, c1910; RIGHT: Tithe Barn (next to the Vicarage), demolished in 1901; CENTRE LEFT; old Wesleyan Chapel, Chapel Hill, and RIGHT: Baptist Chapel, Otley Street, opened June 1861; BELOW: old Congregational Chapel, demolished 1838.

ABOVE: Foundation stones of the New Congregational Church, laid 19 September 1914 by Messrs T.H. Dewhurst, J. Harrison, J.E. Gaunt and Mrs Gunnell; BELOW: Friends Meeting House, the Ginnel; INSET: datestone above the door; OPPOSITE LEFT: the first Primitive Methodist Chapel in Lower Commercial Street from 1835-1880, later a 'cycle shop and until 1974, the Fire Station; RIGHT: the second Primitive Methodist Chapel, Gargrave Road; built 1878 and now replaced by a block of flats; CENTRE: St Monica's Convent, Gargrave Road, and BELOW: a final look at High Street, before Wilson's Statue was moved, in 1921.

ABOVE: Skipton British School, 1908 and BELOW: a contemporary
school group.

For the Children

In 1475 Peter Toller, a substantial landowner in the district became Dean of Craven, and in the same year he established a charity of St Nicholas in the Parish Church. Toller died in 1492, leaving his lands to this charity 'to the intent to pay for his soul and all Christian souls, and to help to do and maintain divine service in the said cure, and also to keep a Grammar School for the children of the same town'.

Shortly after the Dissolution of the Monasteries, in 1545, the charity lands at Skipton were seized, and a continuance warrant provided for an annuity of £4 4s 10d to be paid to the charity. The Skipton lands were granted for the endowment of the Clitheroe Royal Grammar School.

Skipton Grammar School was re-founded in 1548 by William Ermysted, who became a canon residentiary at St Paul's, and Master of the Temple.

In 1555 the 'Clerk's School' was founded: the duties of the Master were to find and maintain one clerk sufficiently learned to teach children to spell and read the ABC, the Primer and Psalter in Latin and not in English, and to teach them to sing plain song perfectly, free of any charge 'except one penny of every scholar at the entry to put his name in the school master's book, and if the scholar has not a penny to let him enter for nothing freely'. The appointment of the clerk was in the hands of the Schoolmaster of the Grammar School, the Vicar, and two of the eldest churchwardens. The Clerk's School was held in the little School house in the churchyard.

The 1548 Foundation Deed of the Grammar School is a much more detailed and comprehensive document. The right of appointment of the Master was in the hands of the Vicar and churchwardens, but if they did not appoint within one month, the right passed to the Master and Fellow of Lincoln College, Oxford, again for one month, otherwise to the Dean and Chapter of St Paul's. This school was kept in a house in Skipton which Ermysted had recently purchased from Henry, 2nd Earl of Cumberland. The school was to be held from 6am to 6pm, with an interval of two hours at mid-day in the summer, and from 7am to 6pm in the winter.

Christopher Petyt, Lord Thanet's Steward at Skipton Castle, wrote to Thomas, the 'Good Earl' in 1723, reporting that the Trustees of the School had met, and examined all the parents of boys at the school 'whereby your Lordship will plainly see how grossly the school-master has neglected his duty'. The Archbishop of York held a Visitation at Skipton in June 1722; 'It plainly appeared to his Grace that the school-master had been guilty of very great negligence in relation to his management of the school, there are not above 15 boys in the whole now at school. He reprimanded Mr Leadal [the master] very severely on this occasion, and his Grace told him he deserved to be turned out, and that if he did not for the future at all times strictly perform his duty in every particular (as in conscience and judgment he ought to do) and with all diligence to raise the credit of the school his Grace assured him he would upon the first complaint against him advise and join with your Lordship and the other Feoffees to displace him, which they have lawful power to do. Mr Leadal then promised a strict and diligent performance of his duty in all respects'. Richard Leadal died in 1724.

In case the nomination should fall on them, Lincoln College, Oxford, made enquiries about a suitable candidate. On 19 March 1727, John Wesley wrote to his mother:

'A school in Yorkshire, 40 miles from Doncaster, was proposed to me lately, on which I shall think more about when it appears I may have it or not. A good salary is annexed to it; so that in a year's time 'tis probable all my debts would be paid and I should have money beforehand. But what has made me wish for it most is the frightful description, as they call it, some gentlemen who know the place gave me of it yesterday. The town (Skipton in Craven) lies in a little vale, so pent up between two hills that it is scarcely accessible on any side; so that you can expect little company from without, and within there is none at all'.

But the Vicar and Churchwardens appointed Rev William Banks as Master, within the time limited, and Lincoln College had no further interest.

Rev Matthew Wilkinson, School Master since 1730, died in 1751. There were two candidates for the vacancy. By judicious bribery, Rev Stephen Barrett secured eight votes, but then got cold feet. He wrote to the Vicar of Carleton: 'The contributing to the worst of national vices is what I abhor, and I think the giver is almost equally immerst in guilt with the receiver'.

When Barrett withdrew, Lincoln College stepped in, and nominated Rev Samuel Plomer. Two new candidates appeared, Rev George Chamberlain and Rev Thomas Carr, each of whom bought six votes — a dead heat. Carr locked all the doors to keep Plomer out of the school; to resolve the impasse it seems that Carr withdrew, with a promise of the succession on Plomer's death in 1780.

The Curate at Skipton Parish Church, Rev Richard Withnell, was appointed. He rushed off to York to procure the Archbishop's licence to teach; the Archbishop claimed the right to examine as to Withnell's religion, morals and learning before granting the licence; Withnell refused to be examined as to his 'learning'; and the Archbishop refused the licence. Litigation followed, and in his judgment the Lord Chief Justice, Lord Kenyon, declared:

'Whoever will examine the state of the grammar schools in different parts of this Kingdom will see to what a lamentable condition most of them are reduced, and would wish that those who have any superintendence or control over them had been as circumspect as the Archbishop of York has been on the present occasion. If other persons had equally done their duty, we should not find, as is now the case, empty walls without scholars, and everything neglected but the receipt of the salaries and emoluments'.

In the meantime, Lincoln College had stepped in again, and appointed Rev Thomas Gartham. His relations with the Vicar and Churchwardens remained frigid, and in January 1822 a public meeting was called to consider how to render the school a useful and efficient establishment. It was decided to draw up a memorial praying the Vicar and Churchwardens to remove Gartham from his office. The charges against him were that for 20 years, the inhabitants had been denied the benefit they should have received from the school, owing to the gross, immoral character of the Master. He had frequently been arrested for debt; had been guilty of 'eccentricity of ideas respecting the course of studies and plan of teaching to be pursued'; and had frequently offered himself in marriage to certain of the petitioners' daughters without any previous acquaintance. There were only 16 children in the school — all except two were children of persons in humble stations of life. Before the new proceedings were settled, Gartham died in December 1824.

A new Constitution laid down in 1841 provided that Latin was still to be a compulsory subject. It seems that, since Gartham's death, Latin had been dropped as a compulsory subject, and more English and arithmetic introduced; Rev William Sidgwick, the Master, said that if the choice of education was left entirely with the parents, the school in a few years would be filled with none but English scholars, many of whom would be sent to obtain the mere elements of English and arithmetic which they might easily obtain at the National School; 'If the Mathematics and Latin are insisted upon it will be the means of making this school more respectable and many persons will be induced to send their children to the said school who do not at present'.

The Vicar and Churchwardens in 1836 petitioned for a new Scheme. This petition began; 'That the School is very old, ill ventilated and lighted and of insufficient size, and your petitioners are advised that it would be beneficial to the Charity to pull it down and erect a new one'. Another new scheme, under the Endowed Schools Act 1869, was formed in 1871, providing for 14 Governors.

In 1877 the School moved from its Newmarket Street site, to a new building erected in Gargrave Road; in the previous year Rev E.T. Hartley had been appointed Headmaster. Under the Education Act 1944, the School obtained 'aided' status.

The Headmasters since 1947 have been: Marselis Lyeendert Forster, 1937-1957; Jack D. Eastwood, 1957-1972; John Woolmore, 1972-1982; and David M. Buckroyd, 1982.

The Sunday School system was set on foot in Gloucester by Robert Raikes in 1770. He himself described the children whom he was trying to educate, albeit in a rudimentary fashion, as 'idle, ungovernable, profligate and filthy in the extreme'. A national Society for the establishment of Sunday Schools throughout the Kingdom was established in 1775.

The Skipton Parish Church Sunday School commenced on 1 January 1776, meeting in the Court House or Tolbooth in Middle Row; the scholars marched to the Church, and the teachers were paid 1s 6d per day. Expenses were met by voluntary subscriptions.

The National School was opened in 1814, and the scholars moved there.

Mrs Catherine Cowman kept a Dame School in Spencer's Yard. She taught reading and writing in the Sunday School. Miss Wimberley, who came from Doncaster, kept a private school in Skipton in 1820 and advertised: 'Ladies Seminary, Skipton-in-Craven. Impressed with gratitude for the favours they have already received, the Misses Wimberley beg to offer their sincere thanks to the generous supporters of their establishment, assure them as was the practice in general that in the discharge of their important Duties, their utmost abilities shall be exerted, when they hope to merit a continuance of their Confidence, which they have hitherto experienced'.

On 15 January 1825 Robert Hume Mossman married a Miss Wimberley and advertised: 'R.H. Mossman, having publicly announced my intention of leaving Skipton, it is necessary to acquaint you that the pressing solicitations of my friends to remain in my present situation, have induced me to comply with their request. I therefore take the liberty to petition a continuance of the very liberal and respectable Patronage with which, for the last five years, I have been honoured '.

In June 1824 William Spencer sold to Martin Luther Gill a warehouse with room over, used as a school in the occupation of Mr Mossman. In July 1826 Mrs Mossman had relinquished the Newmarket Street School in favour of her sister, and Mr Mossman had established himself as the 'Classical and Mathematical School, Preston'.

The Parish Church Sunday School began on 1 January 1786; it is significant that the 'High Mill' was built in 1785, and one of the partners, Christopher Sidgwick (1804-77), had a profound interest in education. He retired early from the partnership in 1833, and devoted himself to Christ Church, which was built 1837-39.

It was decided to build a new 'National School'. Writing to the Earl of Thanet in 1816, the promoters set forth the objects of the proposed school: 'to teach the children of the poor subordination and order, and to train them up in habits of industry and cleanliness'.

Another consideration was factory legislation. In the Factories Bill of 1833, factory owners were required to employ children in the nine to 13 age bracket only if a teacher certified that the child had received two hours' education for six out of the seven days of the previous week. This was never passed, but it was obvious that some legislation would come, and the Factories Act 1844 required children to attend school on a half-time basis for five days a week. In the following year the British School, Christ Church School and Wesleyan Methodist School were all opened.

A number of private schools were springing up. Henry Alcock (b1791) learned his ABC in the Sunday School in Spencer's Yard under Mrs Catherine Cowman. In about 1835 Henry Alcock kept a sedan chair, which was generally used to take his two daughters to a school kept by Miss

Wimberley in Lascelles Hall. They were carried by two footmen, who wore plush knee-breeches with canary-coloured waistcoats and cutaway swallow-tail coats.

From 1786 to 1814 some or all of the scholars met in the old Town Hall (often used as a Court-room), where John and Ann Brown used to officiate as master and mistress: the wages were 1s 6d per day. The children marched from the Court-room to the Church.

Most nonconformist chapels were opened in the 1840s and Sunday Schools soon followed. The earliest of these was the Congregational (Independent) School, (which became known as the 'British School'). The Chapel was built in Newmarket Street in 1839, and John Dewhurst provided a temporary schoolroom in 1844.

Christ Church, Skipton, was built between 1837 and 1839, and a Sunday School was commenced shortly after this. Some years previously Mr Christopher Sidgwick had begun a week-day and Sunday class of boys and girls at the High Mill.

Christopher Sidgwick (1804-1877) was the third son of William Sidgwick; he had been a partner in the High Mill, but he retired young from the cotton mill in 1833, and devoted his energies and his fortune to building and endowing Christ Church.

In about 1838 he had begun a week-day and Sunday class of boys and girls at the High Mill. He engaged a school-mistress to teach the day-school, and he himself conducted the Sunday class. In those days mills 'shut down' at eight pm, and after that long day's work, those who wished to improve themselves gave one and a half or two hours to the schools, and Mr Sidgwick, after his day's work, was always with them. He was exceedingly regular and attentive to his duties, and although at one time he resided at Stone Gappe, some five miles distant from the mill, he invariably reached it on foot at the proper hour for commencing work in Skipton, being very frequently as early as five o-clock in the morning.

The room at the High Mill became in course of time too small for his increasing class of scholars, for Christopher strove to get as many as possible of the children who worked at his factory to improve themselves by attending the night school. He therefore built a two-storied cottage, intending one room for boys, and the other for the girls, and engaged both a master and a mistress. This in turn proving too small, in about 1840 he built a bungalow to house the school-room in Water Street. This was built and maintained at his own expense, except that his brother James contributed £200. He conducted a Sunday School in the same room. This was continued for some time, the scholars attending Christ Church on Sundays.

The land which was to form the site of the bungalow, in Wood's Map of 1832 is shown as the property of J.B. Sidgwick Esq. On 30 December 1840 J.B. Sidgwick conveyed to his brother Christopher for £108 15s 0d a plot of land, a parcel of the Kiln Garth containing 571 square yards 'upon which plot of land Christopher Sidgwick has lately erected and built a school'.

In 1844 Christ Church School (generally known as Croft School) was built; soon after this the Water Street School was given up and the scholars were removed to Christ Church.

A.C. Benson wrote a biography of his great-uncle Dr E.W. Benson in 1874, relating that Christopher 'had been a strong Evangelical, a great scholar and thinker in Theology, and became a very High Churchman'. He had built the Church School in Water Street: 'here in the old days he kept his books in a house adjoining the school, and came down from the Castle for service at seven am in Christ Church, and after breakfast retired to this hermitage to read till three, when he returned to the Castle to dine . . . After the Board School came to Skipton, he closed his own school, and converted the great school-room with its timber roof, into his own library . . . I remember a magnificent looking old man, dressed like an old Quaker with a swallow-tailed coat and frilled shirt-front'. Christopher's obituarist wrote: 'His quaint-looking one-storey residence in Water Street was an illustration of the eccentricity of the man. It was a model dwelling-house for health, comfort and cleanliness; there were no pretensions to luxury; the whole of the joiners' fittings throughout the building being plain polished deal; the doors were also painted white'.

Christopher Sidgwick was on the Committee of the Skipton National School (in Otley Street) and in 1838 he took the Superintendence of the Boys' School, following the dismissal of James Hall for continual drunkenness. In September 1839 he and his brother James put forward a resolution which was passed: 'That the boys attending the National School do, after the New Church is consecrated occupy the seats provided for scholars in that school'. At a special meeting in 1839 it was resolved that the boys attending the National School should be taken to the New Church for divine worship, as they could either hear or see in the accommodation provided for them in the Parish Church. An amendment was passed: 'That the children continue to come to the Parish Church'. Christopher Sidgwick promptly resigned.

New Schools: 1845 — National School for Christ Church parish, opened; 1846 — British School, Otley Street, built; 1874 — Parish Church Schools in Otley Street, created; 1880 — Girls High School; 1889 — Girls Endowed School in Gargrave Road, opened; 1909 — Brougham Street Council School, opened; 1911 — Ings Council School, opened; and 1951 — Greatwood Junior School foundation stone laid.

ABOVE: The old Grammar School, Newmarket Street until 1877, and
BELOW: Girls Endowed School, 1930.

OPPOSITE ABOVE LEFT: Ermysted's Grammar School; main block from south, c1916; RIGHT: the view from the south west; CENTRE: the bungalow, Water Street, built 1840 as a school for children at the mills by Christopher Sidgwick; BELOW LEFT: Spencer's Yard, where Mrs C. Cowman kept a Dame School, and RIGHT: Lascelles Hall — the school kept by Miss Wimberley, which Henry Alcock's daughters attended. ABOVE: A somewhat subdued outing, c1905, and BELOW: Skipton Congregational School, built 1846 and known as the British School.

ABOVE: Closed — the Premier Cinema; still open the Plaza, and here, the Regal; BELOW: opened — the new baths in Aireville Park (May 1964).

60

Money

Whitaker illustrates life in the parish of Linton early in the 19th century. This was a farming community, and their way of life is set out with the observation: 'The quantity of money in circulation must have been inconveivably small. One great advantage of these simple habits was that superfluous wealth and abject poverty were equally excluded . . . the wages of the labourers were low, not exceeding 2½ d a day with board'.

All this altered with the development of the lead mines on Grassington Moor; Whitaker was less generous to the miners: 'Excepting what must always be expected, the introduction of manufactories, I do not know a greater calamity than the discovery of lead mines in the neighbourhood'. Frederick Montagu in *Gleanings in Craven* (1838) disagrees with Whitaker's verdict, he wrote of the miners 'they are all hard working, industrious and generally sober men, many of them have large families, and some of them have the fruits of their labour deposited in the Savings Bank'.

John Alcock was in 1732 admitted a solicitor, having been articled to Richard Robinson, the Earl of Thanet's Steward at Skipton Castle. When he retired in 1783 his son, William Alcock, took over the practice. William Alcock had conducted banking transactions 'on the side' for several years. In Settle the Birkbeck and Peart families had also carried on a limited range of banking activities.

They decided to join forces in 1791. There were six foundation partners in the 'Craven Bank'; William Birkbeck and his cousin John Birkbeck (woolcombers); William Alcock (Solicitor); John Peart (Solicitor), William Lawson and Joseph Smith, a London banker.

The 'Skipton Bank' was founded in 1807 by William Sidgwick, Robinson Chippendale, Christopher Netherwood and John Carr, all of whom were account holders in the Craven Bank. On 11 February 1826 the Craven Bank at Settle refused to accept the notes of the Skipton Bank, and there was a general crisis which led to some banks failing. On 14 February 1826, 84 backers signed a Declaration of Support to the Craven Bank: 'We whose names are subscribed do hereby declare our full and entire confidence in the stability of the Craven Bank . . . and having the highest of possible opinion of the Opulence, Integrity and Prudence of the several partners in that Bank we hereby most willingly pledge ourselves to take their notes in payment to any amount whatever'. This list is headed by Lord Ribblesdale and includes Rev John Clapham, Vicar of Ingleton; Rev Rowland Ingham, Vicar of Giggleswick; James B. Garforth of Coniston; Rev Anthony Lister, Vicar of Gargrave; Matthew Wilson of Eshton Hall; J.N. Coulthurst of Gargrave House and Richard H. Roundell of Gledstone.

In 1843 the Craven Bank partners resolved to take proceedings against Christopher Netherwood and his brother if they refused to grant to the Craven Bank 'a sweeping mortgage over all their estates'. The Market Place property was sold to the Craven Bank.

By 1880 the partners were finding a dearth of suitable successors, and perhaps also finding individual responsibility for so large a concern was too great, so they decided on incorporation. The nominal capital of the new Company was £1,200,000 divided into 40,000 shares of £30 each, but only 25,000 shares were issued, half to the former partners and the other half (at a premium of £9) to the public.

Four of the last six partners were among the first directors: John Birkbeck, William Robinson, George Stansfeld and William Alcock — the other two partners, Joseph Birkbeck and Henry Alcock Jnr relinquished all control.

In 1905 George Stansfeld, chairman of the company, died and was succeeded as chairman by Walter Morrison. In the following year the directors of the Craven Bank Ltd amalgamated with the Bank of Liverpool. By virtue of subsequent amalgamations the Bank became Martins Bank in 1928, and is now Barclays Bank.

Speaking at the opening of the new Building Society office in 1928, Philip Snowden said: 'The Building Society movement was one of a number of associated working class movements which had done a great deal, indeed, an incalculable amount of work, to raise the social conditions of the working people of the country. The Building Society movement, and such movements as the Co-operative movement and the Friendly Society movement, all working class in origin, had erected magnificent monuments to the thrift, capacity, ability and spirit of independence of the working people of the country'. The Co-operative movement did not appear in Skipton until 1861, while the Co-operative origin is shrouded beneath a Sunwin store. Savings banks are another movement of the same type, as will be seen from the distinguished gentlemen who became patrons of the Bank.

On Saturday 4 February 1818 a savings bank was established at Skipton, under the designation of the Craven Savings Bank. The Patrons were the Duke of Devonshire and the Earl of Thanet, the Lord Ribblesdale was the President. Stephen Bailey Hall — admitted a Solicitor in 1817 — was Manager of the Savings Bank from its inception until his death in October 1866. The Bank died with him.

Hall is worthy of note as one of the few local poets whose work is at all bearable. His verses are published in a slim volume: '*The Testament of Faith, Israel, Warning to Britain*, and other poems'. These were, he wrote, 'a pleasing employment during the leisure hours of a profession which has generally been deemed unpropitious to such occupation'.

The Skipton and District Permanent Benefit Building Society was established in 1853, and *The Craven Herald* of July 1853 gave the new venture its support: 'A public meeting was lately held in the Town-Hall, for the purpose of establishing a Building Society for Skipton and the surrounding district. After a few preliminary remarks, Mr John Bell, Manager of two of the Leeds building societies, explained the principles and practice of these valuable institutions. He remarked that he had thoroughly examined, and spent a considerable time in an investigation of the principle of these societies, and would unhesitatingly affirm that they were based upon a solid and equitable foundation; and he gave some practical illustrations of the advantages to the working classes in becoming members, and thus imbibing provident habits for the good of their families and the Public'.

The Craven Herald of August 1853 stated that 'Investment in the Society was a good investment, and especially suitable for the weekly savings of the working classes'.

Most of the early Building Societies were societies for developing a particular site. In 1821 the Hart's Head Building Society was responsible for building Queen's Street; it is believed that Union Square was erected on a similar basis, and in 1875 a building club was announced for 53 houses fronting to Broughton Road. These were 'terminating societies' which were wound up on the completion of a particular venture. It was not necessary for a Permanent Society to refer to this permanence in its name, and in 1929 the name of the 'Skipton and District Permanent Building Society' was changed to 'Skipton Building Society'.

The former offices of the Society were in Newmarket Street. In 1927 the Society purchased 'Draper Smiths' shop at 59 High Street. New offices were built on the site. On 15 September 1928 they were opened by the Rt Hon Philip Snowden, a native of Cowling, and ex-Chancellor of the Exchequer.

The Craven Herald stated: 'We think the selection of offices, has been well made, and we are glad to observe, from the names enrolled in the prospectus, that it is actuated by no sectarian or party feeling, but includes in its ranks individuals of all parties in politics, as well as religion. Give a man a stake in the Country, however small, and immediately he becomes in every respect a better member of society'.

With the Society's continued growth over the years, it became obvious in the early seventies that further accommodation would be required at the Head Office in the foreseeable future. After great deliberation, it was eventually decided to demolish some old buildings at the rear of the existing premises, and to build a new extension on the site. By a strange co-incidence, the office which the Society occupied when it was formed in 1853 is part of the site on which the new extension has been erected.

On 30 September 1982 the 'Skipton' took over the assets (then about £24½ million) of the neighbouring Otley Building Society. Both societies had been providing a service in neighbouring market towns for upwards of 130 years, and it was a natural development that they should join forces to form a strong regional Society. This Society is now the largest which is based in the County of North Yorkshire, with a staff of 303, about half of whom comprise the Head Office establishment, with the remainder spread among the 50 branch offices. There are also 77 agency offices in various parts of the country. The assets of the Society as at 31 December 1982 exceeded £313 million.

The nine Directors are all professional and business men in the district. The Secretaries during the present century have been as follows: Joseph Watson, Secretary 1889-1915; Arthur Smith, Secretary 1915-1953; Director 1935-died 1965; Cyril Clarke, joined Society 1924; Secretary 1953-1973 (General Manager 1958) retired 1973 Director 1969 resigned 1979; Harry Taylforth, joined Society 1936, General Manager 1969; Director. March 1979.

LEFT: The Bailey, formerly the home of RIGHT: Henry Alcock. (STC)

LEFT: London Midland Bank, Caroline Square, c1900; BELOW: £5 banknote of the Yorkshire Banking Co, and RIGHT: Walter Morrison of Malham Tarn House, (1836-1921), last chairman of the Craven Bank. (STC)

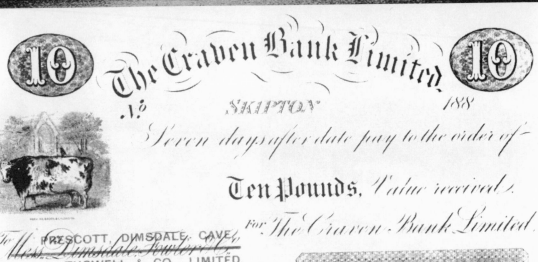

LEFT: Yorkshire Bank 1887; RIGHT: Midland Bank, formerly the Yorkshire Bank; CENTRE: Aireville Hall, built by Henry Alcock c1840, and BELOW: £10 banknote of the Craven Bank and showing the Craven Heifer.

ABOVE: Draper Smith's shop in High Street, purchased by Skipton
Building Society in 1927 for new offices; LEFT: the Craven Bank
amalgamated with the Bank of Liverpool and Martins Ltd, later Martins
Bank; RIGHT: Skipton Building Society, after alterations to the frontage,
opened by Philip Snowden, 1928.

66

Riot and Retribution

In the early 'Hungry Forties' of the last century, there was a great trade depression, particularly acute in the North, which textile operatives attributed to power-looms, but was also due to the Corn Laws, to the need for increased capital in manufacturing, or to the state of the currency, according to your political predilection. As Harbutt Dawson neatly puts it: 'The textile operatives of East Lancashire did not bear their troubles with the fortitude that characterised their near Yorkshire neighbours'. The workers of Burnley visited Colne, urging the Colne operatives to come to Skipton and prevail upon the Skiptonians to march to Addingham, and so inflame the entire neighbourhood. Their objects were to draw the plugs from the waggon-boilers at the mills, so letting out the water and extinguishing the fire; and also to beg food, as many of them were nearly starving; 'begging food' inevitably became 'demanding food' and demanding 'protection money' and led to some looting.

On Tuesday 16 August 1842 — a hot, sunny, summer's day — a crowd of some 3,000 men, women and children left Colne for Skipton. *En route*, they called on the hand-loom weavers who gave Barnoldswick and Earby their staple industry, and took away their shuttles to immobilise the looms. One party visited Gargrave and stopped the mills there, and the whole contingent then converged on Skipton. Five-year-old Joseph Platt (1837-1927) was to recall his fright when the plug-drawers called at Aireville Grange and demanded milk from his mother. One old lady recalled how, on the afternoon of Tuesday 16 August, she and her sister saw bodies of men, accompanied by women and children, advancing up Broughton Road, marching four abreast, and armed with heavy sticks. These sticks they carried horizontally, each man holding a stick by the end — in this way presenting a solid front to an attacking party. The leaders were distinguished by a white band round the arm.

The magistrates — Mathew Wilson sen, Mathew Wilson jnr (later Sir Mathew), Cooper Preston, James Braithwaite Garforth, Hastings Ingham and Thomas Birkbeck — had received advance notice of the invasion and had taken the precaution of swearing in a large number of special constables to assist the Parish Constable, old Tommy Lowcock.

Mr Ingham and Mr Birkbeck met the rioters, and a parley took place between Ingham and William Smith, the spokesman for the operatives, who explained that their object was to stop the mills and turn out the operatives: the contemporary name for the disturbances was the 'Turn-Out Riots'. Ingham (then 34 years of age — he died aged 91 in 1900) pointed out that the people of Skipton were much alarmed, and begged the Lancastrians not to resort to violence, or to enter any shops or houses; Smith assured the magistrates that they had no intention to injure life or property.

It was quite impossible to prevent the mob from entering the town (there were 3,000 from Colne and under 5,000 inhabitants of Skipton), so Ingham rode on to Colne to call out the military. In his absence some 300 or 400 rioters visited first Dewhurst's Mill, then Sidgwick's newly opened Low Mill, and then Sidgwick's High Mill, in each of which they drew off the water from the engines, stopping the working of the mills. Christopher Sidgwick, who had retired from the family firm in 1833, was an attentive witness to their conduct at the High Mill. William Paget, the Clerk to Solicitor Thomas Brown, was (surely not fortuitously), at both the Sidgwick Mills, and later testified that

67

the rioters were at first driven back from the High Mill. After drawing the plugs, Smith ordered the workmen to be turned out, and the mill to be kept standing until the delegates at Manchester had determined the rate of wages, and there were threats that if the mill re-opened without the plug-drawers' consent, they would return and do further mischief. The crowd then asked for money, and one of them said it was usual for mill-owners to give money. Sidgwick asked who was the leader, and Smith was put forward. Sidgwick promised to pay a sovereign after the crowd had left the mill, if they would not return; Smith ordered the crowd to go away, and the mill yard was cleared in about a quarter of an hour. The sovereign was then paid.

According to Dawson, while the mills were being immobilised, 'other parties went round the town levying blackmail, entering shops and houses, and carrying away all the food on which they could lay their hands, and demanding money. There was a perfect panic amongst the inhabitants. Business was entirely suspended; shops were shut, while the windows of private houses were closed, and the doors in many places securely fastened. In a multitude of instances householders had provided food against their coming, knowing this to be one of their demands'.

Finally, in response to Ingham's appeals, a company of the 61st Regiment of Foot and a party of the 11th Hussars, under the command of Captain Jones, arrived in the town after a march of less than three hours in the sweltering heat. The magistrates decided that the time had come to read the Riot Act, and from the Town Hall steps in Sheep Street Mathew Wilson jnr, read the following proclamation:

'Our Sovereign Lady the Queen chargeth and commandeth all persons being assembled immediately to disperse themselves, and peaceably to depart to their habitations and to their lawful business, upon the pains contained in an Act made in the first year of King George for preventing tumultuous and riotous assemblies. God Save the Queen'.

Under the Riot Act 1716 it is a felony to continue together for one hour after the proclamation is read, and the justices are required to seize and apprehend all persons continuing after the hour — which they were clearly unable to do. Mathew Wilson's proclamation had no effect, the crowd did not disperse, so Hastings Ingham mounted his horse and read the proclamation in every part of the town.

Then an old and respected timber merchant, John Settle, offered to lend the rioters one of his fields, and to provide them with beer and refreshments. It is not known whether this arose out of sympathy, or whether Settle's objective was to clear the streets and leave the rioters in an exposed position, where the military could with ease disperse them. The field was known as Anna Hills; it was the site of Skipton Old Station and now of Hillard's Supermarket.

The magistrates followed the mob to Anna Hills, and Ingham again read the Riot Act in various parts of the field. The mob still refused to disperse, and indeed threatened to attack the magistrates, who had become temporarily detached from the troops, who had by now arrived. The magistrates therefore ordered the infantry to clear the field. One of them, Cooper Preston of Flasby Hall repeatedly called on the soldiers to 'Fire', but Captain Jones turned to his men, saying: 'No, men, I am your commander' and ordered them to fix bayonets and charge. William Spencer, who had been seen at the mills, called on the crowd to be firm and stand still. The rioters promptly retreated into an adjacent lane, and began throwing stones at the soldiers and the magistrates. There was evidence that William Spencer, John Spencer and James Dakin were among the stone-throwers.

James Braithwaite Garforth JP, was struck on the head, his eyeglasses were dashed to the ground, and his sight seriously impaired. It was said that he was waving his stick above his head, when one of the rioters (believed to be a Barrowford blacksmith) came up and with a heavy club struck him in the face, breaking his spectacles, putting out an eye, and knocking out several of his teeth.

William Smith (46), William Spencer (47), John Spencer (50), John Harland (38), Edward Hey (32) and James Dakin (27) were arrested and conveyed to the Devonshire Hotel for examination by the magistrates. On the following day the six prisoners were committed for trial, charged with having 'with force and arms, together with other evil disposed persons, unlawfully and riotously assembled and gathered to disturb the public peace, and then and there made a great noise, riot and disturbance to the terror of the Queen's subjects, and against the peace of our Lady the Queen'. A coach was provided, and Hastings Ingham and an escort under Captain Jones accompanied the prisoners a mile or two on the York road.

In September the six prisoners came up for trial at the Yorkshire Summer Assize at York before Mr Justice Maule. No evidence was offered against two of them — Harland and Hey — who were discharged. William Smith's counsel claimed that he had led the starving mob in a creditable manner: 'the town was at their mercy, but not the slightest injury was done, either to person or property, except the letting out of water from the boilers of a few engines'. J.B. Garforth would not have agreed.

The Judge's summing-up was virtually a direction to convict: 'If the practice was to be permitted of stopping mills until the delegation at Manchester permitted work to be resumed . . . there would be an end to any government'. The conduct of the magistrates in dispersing 'this most illegal assembly' was proper and commendable, and finally: 'Any person who had joined the mob by whom these illegal acts were perpetrated, although they might not be proved to have taken an active part, still by their presence, they rendered themselves responsible to the law'. According to the Chartist newspaper, the *Northern Star* the Judge went even further: 'He went through the evidence and pointed out the points which were material against the prisoners. He had no doubt that the evidence fully bore out the offence with which the persons were charged'. The Court, he said, was 'deeply indebted to the Government for the leniency they had shown in not prosecuting them for high treason . . . or in having indicted them for robbery, as was the case during the celebrated riots in London, when a poor man asked for relief, and got half a crown, for which he was afterwards hung on a charge of robbery'.

It is surprising that after this charge, the jury took half an hour to bring in a verdict of 'Guilty'. Apparently the delay was due to consideration of whether there should be any recommendation to mercy; the jury could not agree on this, but thought the two Spencers less culpable than the others. William Spencer's plea for leniency on the ground that he had a wife and eight children, went unheeded; Smith, as the ringleader, received a sentence of 12 months' imprisonment with hard labour; the other three convicted men each received a sentence of six months with hard labour.

The first rioters were sentenced on Monday 5 September and on the following Friday at 5am, about six constables were sent to Barnoldswick to arrest John Greenwood (34) and John Hodgson (35). The preliminary hearing was in the Town Hall and evidence was called that both accused had taken a very active part, and had extorted money. They were committed for trial, and remained in prison until the next York Assizes.

On 27 March 1843 they came up for trial, along with Hartley Stansfield (25) who had been out on bail and was charged not only with rioting, but also with assaulting the unfortunate Mr Garforth. All three were found guilty of a riot; Stansfield was acquitted of the assault charge, but as he had confessed before the magistrates that he struck someone with a stick, he was sentenced by Mr Baron Parke to four months' imprisonment with hard labour. Greenwood and Hodgson, who had been in custody for over six months, received a sentence of one month with hard labour.

The maintenance of law and order was ultimately the responsibility of the magistrates, who committed malefactors for trial at the Assize Court or the Quarter Sessions. Market offences, mostly of a trivial nature and concerning public health, were in the hands of the Court Leet, which appointed the Parish Constables. The Charge to the Jury of the Court Leet was as follows:

1st You are to enquire into all High Treasons and petty Treasons, Felonies, together with their accessories, which offences though not punishable here, yet are presentable and the presentment must be certified to the Quarter Sessions. You are to ensure into all public nuisances here and lewd Ale Houses.

2nd You are also to enquire if the highways footpaths and bridges within this Leet be unrepaired if any have erected walls hedges or fences or digged pits in the highways or if any hedge trees or boughs adjoining the highway be uncut gutters unscoured or watercourses stopped or turned out of their ancient course or if the common rivers or watering places be annoyed or thrown in or near the highways or any common watering place.

You are also to enquire if the Constables have discharged their duties and particularly if any have used false weights or measures or if any have killed or destroyed the game within this manor not being qualified or present therein.

It was usual to celebrate Guy Fawkes Day with fireworks and bonfires at the expense of the parish, and the church bells were rung. The anniversary had lost its political significance, but the townspeople continued to discharge fireworks and to carry blazing brushwood through the streets.

Not until the early 1850s was it obligatory for the County Council to appoint a Superintending Constable. In 1852 Superintendent Beanlands issued a notice in strong terms, which was considered by the townspeople to be an infringement of the liberties of the people. Hundreds turned up in High Street, and the celebrations were kept up in a lively manner.

Although it is irrelevant to the problems of Guy Fawkes, it is interesting to note that in 1862 the Chief Constable of the West Riding issued a notice announcing that Mr Hodgson Lewis, a Superintendent in the WR Constabulary, had just absconded from Skipton, after embezzling various sums of money belonging to the magisterial authorities.

In 1872 Superintendent Thomas Grisdale provided another confrontation, when appointed about three years earlier, he announced his determination to bring Skipton to such a highly moral condition that he would be enabled to hang his watch on the parish church gates at night, and find it there the next morning. He never had the confidence to try out this experiment. The Superintendent was determined that on 5 November 1872 Skiptonians should experience the full terror of the law. The town was placarded with notices warning the public against any breach of the peace which might result from their assembling in large crowds and letting off fireworks, and additional constables were drafted in from neighbouring towns.

Instead of the bills having a salutary effect upon the minds of the inhabitants of the town, it was just the contrary, and the people thought it was an interference with their rights and privileges as Englishmen and an act of great impropriety on the part of the Superintendent to curtail these privileges or place a limit on their amusements.

On 5 November 1872 between six and seven pm Grisdale came into the streets, accompanied by Sergeant Carr. In Caroline Square little boys letting off fireworks were ignored. At about eight o'clock the gathering became discreditable and excited stone-throwing began. The police applied to Grisdale and asked him if they were to stand as targets to be shot at and injured without attempting to disperse the crowd. Grisdale went in front and remonstrated as to the attack on the police, and appealed to the crowd to desist. He was pelted with stones.

There was by now a strong body of policemen in the main street. Grisdale applied to J.B. Dewhurst, a magistrate, to read the Riot Act, but he refused. At about 10 o'clock the Christ Church Drum and Fife Band played up the street. The *Keighley News* reported: 'In the dark some peaceable persons got either knocked down or received a blow from a policeman, whilst on the other hand stones in abundance were thrown at the heads of the constables. Seven squares of glass were broken at the Wheat Sheaf Inn, and one very large square in the Post Ofice by stones which the mob threw at the Superindendent and his men. Several persons lost their hats whilst hundreds lost their tempers by being pushed along by the police, and not a few received blows over heads and arms which they will not soon forget. It is reported that the Superintendent of police was punched and struck at. It was long after midnight before the crowd dispersed to their homes'.

At the ensuing Magistrates' Court, Mathew Wilson was in the chair, and Captain McNeill, Chief Constable of the West Riding, attended — an indication of the concern felt by the authorities as to the deterioration of relations between the police and the public. The court was crowded, and when Superintendent Grisdale entered, he was greeted with hisses. The defendants' solicitor 'was compelled to say, though reluctantly, that had it not been for the conduct of Superintendent Grisdale, the disturbances on 5 November would not have taken place; he was a highly respectable and trustworthy man (hisses), but he had acquitted himself in a somewhat injudicious manner'.

Police Sergeant Snowden gave evidence that some fireworks went off as early as five thirty pm and before eight pm stones had been thrown. There were only six police and himself on duty up to seven and near to eight o'clock. After eight o'clock there were about 20 police on duty. When the police came on duty about six o'clock there were a few hundreds on the streets. There were about 2,000 or 3,000 people about when he saw the defendant, Joseph Barker, throw a stone. The charge of breach of the peace was found proved, and Barker was find 20s and costs. The same penalty for the same offence was imposed on William Baldwin, Ovington Butler and Abraham Varley. The decisions were greeted with hisses in court. The case against J.T. Parkinson for letting off fireworks was withdrawn on payment of costs.

PC Metcalfe was charged with an assault on John Staveley. The case was dismissed (hisses). Superintendent Grisdale got up on the form on which he had been seated, and shouted: 'Constables, the first man who creates a noise or disturbance you must take into custody'.

In the 'Editor's Notes' column in the next issue of the *Craven Pioneer* appeared the statement: 'Mr Grisdale, our Superintendent of Police, has left us, and Sergeant Carr, formerly stationed at Skipton is, we understand, in charge until the appointment of a successor. Less than one short week sufficed to tarnish the reputation of our town, and to render the removal of our Superintendent a necessary and judicious act'.

One aggrieved citizen, Edward Bradley, brought an action for damages in Skipton County Court, which was heard in March 1873. He was unable to work for more than a fortnight afterwards, and had to be attended by a medical man, Dr Granger, who charged him 14s 6d. One John Stephenson deposed that he distinctly saw the Superintendent knock the plaintiff down. The defendant denied the offence altogether, and a number of policemen stated that the defendant did not knock the plaintiff down, saying that he was knocked down by two strange policemen whose names were not known. The jury gave a verdict for £2 14s 6d. The judge (Judge Daniel QC) refused to order costs, presumably to express his opinion as to the merits of the case.

Skipton Old Station — on the site of Anna Hills, where the Plug Drawing Riots took place.

ABOVE LEFT: The steps in Sheep Street leading to the old Town Hall where Mathew Wilson junior (magistrate, later Sir Mathew) read the Riot Act; RIGHT: J.B. Dewhurst, JP; (STC) BELOW LEFT: the statue of Sir Mathew Wilson, Baronet, MP for the West Riding of Yorkshire, northern division 1874-1885, and first MP for the Skipton division of Yorkshire (1885-1886), in front of the church gates; RIGHT: statue of Sir Mathew, ready for removal to the front of the library in 1921.

ABOVE: Skipton Hospital, and an anything but riotous 1901 Gala
Committee; BELOW: Coronation arch for a peaceful gathering, at Ship
Corner, 1911.

ABOVE:An orderly Coronation march past, June 22, 1911 and BELOW:
a tranquil market day spreads down the Keighley Road in the '20s.

Warp and Weft

Hand-loom weaving was the principal industry in Skipton until the Victorian era. Many houses erected in the first half of the 19th century were built specifically for hand-loom weavers; they were three-storey houses, the top floor being intended as a weaving loft. All the houses in Union Square were built in this fashion.

When William Sidgwick gave evidence before the Select Committee on the state of the children employed in the manufactories of the UK in 1816, he was asked whether the hand-loom weavers were sometimes in the habit of drinking one part of the week, and of working most laboriously the remaining part of it. He had known the weavers, when the wages had been great, play on Monday and Tuesday, and then work on Wednesday, Thursday and Friday, during half the night, take their work home on Saturday, receive their money, and then go to drink again.

At a Meeting of Tradesmen of the West Riding held in Leeds in 1841 John Metcalfe, one of the Skipton representatives, said that in his own district the small class of manufacturers was rapidly going into decay, and the hand-loom weavers were severely depressed. There was one species of cloth woven, of which 30 yards were produced for 4d, and an able-bodied man must work both night and day for a week, in order to produce ten pieces, which would leave him the miserable pittance of 3s 4d for the support of himself and family.

The Leeds Mercury in February 1809 notes: 'there is perhaps not a town in the West Riding feels the pressure of the present calamitous times, more than Skipton-in-Craven. The poor (who are numerous) and are principally supported by the manufacture of cotton have not half work and that they have is at very reduced prices: in the weaving department 2s 9d is paid for what in flourishing times brought 10s'.

The first mill in Skipton was the High Mill, at the entrance to the Castle Woods, built by Peter Garforth, John Blackburn and John Sidgwick in 1785. This was engaged in spinning cotton yarn on wooden frames, the mill being turned by water. Initially a day shift and a night shift were employed, but this did not last long as the water supply was not adequate. A later part of the mill, turned by steam, was built in 1825.

At the Select Committee Enquiry in 1816, on the proposed regulations as to hours of work and ages of children, the substance of the masters' justification was threefold: (1) A man who works 12 hours cannot produce so much work as a man who works 13 hours. Any reduction in hours was a present to foreign manufacturers. (2) This is not laborious work, it is more a matter of attention than of labour. (3) Families are often dependent on the wages of their children, and it would be a hardship to them if children were laid off; the parents would conceive it a loss of their British birthright, that of a parent over his child.

Similar sentiments were expressed by J.B. Sidgwick in 1834, when he told the Factory Committee that corporal punishment had been inflicted by the overseer with his knowledge. He had not forbidden it 'nor do I intend to do so, as I think it would be to the injury of the child to be allowed to do wrong, and not be punished, and to the injury of the parents as he must then be dismissed from the mill'.

Dawson in his *History* wrote in 1882 that 'weaving is now done at the High Mill upon a small scale in addition to spinning'. He later wrote that the mill was abandoned, because the lease fell in and could not be negotiated again.

John Dewhurst built Belle Vue Mills in Broughton Road in 1828, and the mill was run for the first time on 17 February 1829, for worsted spinning and weaving. This mill was burned to the ground on Sunday 2 January 1831, and rebuilt within a year, now as a cotton mill. 'It is a circumstance illustrative of the popular feeling of that time', wrote Dawson 'that the looms were brought with absolute secrecy, and securely boxed up, so that it might not be known what they were'.

In 1852 the mill was greatly extended, and a shed to hold 385 looms was added. In 1863-4 a warehouse was erected on the site of the old workhouse. During the years 1867-70 the newest and largest mill, a 'noble building' adjacent to Broughton Road, was erected.

The main building is 225 feet in length and 70 ft 8 ins in width. It is five storeys high. The entire factory premises of Dewhursts have a floor area of 20,000 square yards. More than 800 operatives were in continual employment (in 1882). Dewhursts were engaged in the spinning and weaving of cotton, and in the manufacture of sewing cotton, all the varied processes, including dyeing, being performed on the premises. Dewhursts became 'The Home of Sylko'.

In 1886 electric light was installed at Belle Vue Mill. About 100 Swan incandescent lamps were hung in the new building and the weaving shed.

In 1888 the family business was converted into a private limited company — John Dewhurst & Sons Ltd — all five directors being named Dewhurst.

Fourteen firms combined in 1897 to form the English Sewing Cotton Co Ltd, the first Chairman of which (1897-1902) was Algernon Dewhurst, son of John Bonny Dewhurst. The 14 firms included Dewhursts of Skipton, and Rickards of Skipton (Low Mill) and Bell Busk.

A major blow fell in February 1983: English Sewing Cotton Co Ltd, announced that they were closing their operation in Skipton by August. This would mean the loss of 240 jobs.

Built in 1839 in Sackville Street by John Benson Sidgwick and Robert Hodgson Sidgwick for weaving and weft spinning, Low Mill was sold in about 1896 to C.A. Rickards Ltd of Airton, who adapted it for the manufacture of silk. The mill soon became known as the Silk Mill. There was an alarm of fire in 1876, but damage was averted by the promptness of the 'hands' without the fire engine having to be called. A more serious fire occurred on 19 November 1908, of which the *Craven Herald* told the story.

The Manager, Mr Hollies sent for two mechanics who lived in Skipton to inspect a loose segment, in a wheel, which was rattling. They were just ready for starting when Hollies called to Walter Taylor to stand back. As he did so the flame from a lamp which he (Walter Taylor) was holding caught the fluff on the wheel and a blaze flared up immediately. Burning silk — light and inflammable — fell on the oil-saturated driving belt, the blaze ran up to the ceiling, and before anything could be done the room was enveloped in flames. The engine tenter was sent off to sound the fire alarm. At 4.40 am the Skipton fire engine was ready for action; the Firth Shed Voluntary Brigade was already there. At 6.15 am the roof gave way. The mill was gutted. The loss (happily insured) was estimated at £30,000.

The most disastrous fire in Skipton for many years resulted in the demolition of the mill, and the taking away from about 300 people of their means of livelihood: 'in the present depressed condition of the trade, it is improbable that they will obtain employment at the other manufacturing establishments in the town'.

The Silk Mill was not re-erected but a new mill known as Sackville Mill was built on substantially the same site. This is now occupied by the Yorkshire Water Authority.

One of Skipton's potential poets recorded the fire:

'I am sure you well remember
That on the 19th of November
The old mill was burned to the ground
The firemen from the station
Came with great ex... tion
But the specta... on in silence all around.'

Samuel Farey, a man of ... Skipton from Kettering in 1844 to take up the
post of Master of the ... d there for 22 years. He was the first Skipton
teacher to recei...

He disag... oper remuneration, and left the school to
establish him... e school by his son-in-law Alfred Gunnell,
who also gave... nnected with S. Farey and Son.

Samuel Fare... William Richard Gibbs Farey in 1906
made a substant... 200 further looms, in addition to the
original 300 loom... adford and Manchester trade were
made here. On the ... st Sam'. He also became a member
of Skipton Building ... 1853, served as Secretary from
1856 to 1888, and as ...

Sam Farey had no pr... ll connected with the Dewhurst
family, who virtually pa... urch and the British School.
When he died in 1895, at ... Church. His son, William,
took over the business, in ... served on Skipton Urban
District Council from 1895 t... 11. He was unfortunately
going blind, and had to be n...

W.R.G. Farey died in 1925, a... e a councillor in 1962,
Chairman in 1968-9 and Mayor...

Unhappily W.R.G. Farey coul... twenties; the Bank
appointed a Receiver and Manager, ... Mark Nutter Ltd,
who had been in business in Nelson ... ings was built up
by selling to makers-up direct, and conc... roduced, along
with umbrella cloths, curtains and dow... achute fabric.

In about 1964, though Mark Nutter L... the property
and business as a going concern, at its full... nary shares
were sold to Hindley Bros, who took over the... eys wished
to sell their asset, and a sale to Carrington and ... property
passed to Carrington-Viyella.

Firth Shed was last used for weaving in Dece... operty
was then sold to Merritt and Fryers Ltd.

Meanwhile Peter Robinson had come to Skipton ... tter
Furnishings. He left the Company in about 1969 t... as
International Textile Co Ltd. At first he took premis... s
Road, and from there he moved to the former offices of ...
there since with remarkable success. In 1981 he was prese...

Park Shed, near the junction of Newmarket Street, w...
and is still often referred to as 'Wilkinson's Mill'. Throug...
on the Leeds and Liverpool Canal, but Park Shed was buil...
and bleaching plant was added later.

The Mill was originally let to F. Pickles and Co; on Mr Pickle...

The Mill was in two parts — the mill fronting to Brougham Street which occupied about two thirds of the buildings, and a new portion in Shortbank Road, which was at one time occupied by Reckitt and Sons Ltd, and is now occupied by Castle Acoustics.

In 1961 Thomas Wilkinson's company sold the front portion to Garner Prestwich Ltd. It is now let (according to the name-plates) to Annmed Marketing Ltd, Annmed Import and Export Ltd, Planmoor, Pennymill Fabrics Co and Interiors (Skipton). These premises provide warehousing, packaging and showroom facilities.

The Skipton Mill Company was incorporated in 1866 with a nominal capital of £20,000 in £5 shares. The Managing Director was John Haigh of West View Terrace, and the Secretary was M.R. Knowles, solicitor.

In the same year (1866) the company built a large shed, Union Mill, by the side of the canal opposite the land known as 'The Firth'. They extended this in 1876 and room was now available for 800 looms. The goods manufactured were winceys, stripes, and checks. The promoters, (according to Dawson) referred to their projected company as the 'Skipton Cotton Company Ltd' but 'Skipton Mill Co Ltd' was shorter and more convenient. Many years later this company sold the Union Shed to its tenants. In Skipton the names 'Mill' and 'Shed' are interchangeable. 'Shed' is a name coined in Lancashire.

In 1897, Broughton Road Mill was built by the Skipton Room and Power Co Ltd, which had been formed with a capital of £20,000 in £5 shares. The directors were W.H. Atkinson (Managing), J.C. Fell (Chairman), T. Duckett, J.H. Hartley, D. Jones and G.H. Mason. The Secretary was Joseph Watson, also the Secretary of Skipton Building Society.

Shortly after five am on 30 March 1958 a fire was discovered, and within a short space of time the mill was ablaze from end to end. Flames shot as high as 50 ft above the building, and could be seen for miles around. Families living in Marton Street were evacuated, then the side of the mill collapsed, and huge stones crashed through the windows of several houses. The blaze was so fierce that lead flashing melted around the chimneys of these houses. Thirteen fire brigades were in action, fighting to prevent the blaze from spreading to the weaving sheds behind the main building. In this they were happily successful and Rycroft and Hartley were able to resume operations after only a few weeks.

The mill was then occupied by Rycroft and Hartley, the second largest manufacturing firm in Skipton; and by Garner Prestwich, who employed a staff of 120, and who moved to other premises after the fire.

The neighbours offered practical help. The Broughton Road Methodist Church placed their Sunday School — known throughout Skipton as the 'tin tab' — at the disposal of Rycroft and Hartley Ltd. This company was incorporated in 1911. In about 1956 it became a branch of Taylor and Hartley, Westhoughton, nr Manchester.

Mr Rawson Rycroft and Mr Wm H. Rycroft were joint directors and general managers of Rycroft and Hartley, the other local directors being Mr John P. Rycroft and Mr E. Platt. In 1958 they employed over 200 work-people.

The list of subscribers is interesting: T.P. Brown, Solicitor and Coroner, £4,000 for 200 shares at £5 each; Lord Hothfield took up 40 shares; Joseph Watson 20 shares and Wm Harbutt Dawson 40 shares.

Dawson (1882) has a brief paragraph about Alexandra Mill: 'Mr George Walton in 1877-8 built for himself a large shed on the canal bank in Keighley Road, beyond the Old Toll-bar, and in June of the later year first ran machinery there. The premises comprise weaving shed (holding 500 looms); warehouses, weft-room, engine and boiler houses, finishing room and offices, and they stand upon 3,300 square yards of ground. The building is now occupied by two firms — Mr G. Walton (the owner) and Messrs Walton Hainsworth & Co. Here are manufactured dress goods, skirtings and shirtings'.

Later Dawson adds a further note: 'In the meantime a series of energetic individual adventurers had appeared on the scene. One of the earliest was George Walton, who brought to the town, in addition to an active interest in public affairs, a spirit of enterprise which materialised in the building in 1877-8 of the large "Alexandra" weaving shed on the canal bank in Keighley Road . . . a speculation which was amply justified by its success'.

Formerly known as the Soke-Mill, the High Corn Mill on Chapel Hill is referred to in a valuation of 1310. The tenants within the Manor of Skipton were bound to have their corn ground at this mill, and to pay a 'mulcture toll'.

The inhabitants disputed the obligations of the Castle tenants, and a number of them set up their own steel mills for grinding their own corn; Benjamin Smith, in Sheep Street, not only used to grind his own corn, but he carted his steel mill from door to door for his own private gains. The owner of the corn mill thought it prudent to inform the bailiff of the manor (nephew to Benjamin Smith) that he would no longer be employed as bailiff unless he brought pressure on his uncle to encourage him to desist from using the steel mill. Benjamin Smith desisted.

The Earl of Thanet won an action to prevent any further breach of the Corn Mill's monopoly, and in the 19th century he lifted the 'malt money' or toll.

In 1954 Skipton Castle Estates sold their properties, and George Leatt became the owner of the Corn Mill, who now maintains the George Leatt Industrial and Folk Museum. Since 1965 George Leatt has begun the task of restoration and repair, and installation of many machines, all driven by water wheels. The Museum is normally open to the public from noon at a small charge.

Aerial view of Dewhurst's mill, with Union Square, built in early 1800s,
in the right hand bottom corner.

LEFT: Mill Bridge; ABOVE: the old Pinder Bridge, and CENTRE; in 1908; BELOW: Skipton Fire Brigade, 1905.

High Mill, Skipton Woods spinners, 1868.

ABOVE LEFT: Dewhurst's mill and mill chimney, Midland Hotel on the left; RIGHT: Broughton Road and Dewhurst's mill; BELOW: Broughton Road mill, which was severely damaged by fire in 1958.

LEFT: entrance to BELOW: Union Square, demolished in 1956. (Note the three storeyed houses, the top storey being reserved for hand loom weaving); RIGHT; fire at the Silk Mill, 19 November 1908.

ABOVE: The Silk Mill fire of 19 November 1908; BELOW: inside Park Mill at the Coronation; OPPOSITE LEFT: Victoria Mill; RIGHT: R.H. Sidgwick, who built the Low Mill with J.B. Sidgwick, and who was the third Chairman of the old Skipton Urban Council; BELOW: retail trade put its wares on display here in Keighley Road.

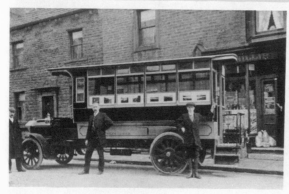

ABOVE LEFT: Carrying cotton waste (George Dawson, centre); RIGHT: the brewery dray in Otley Street; CENTRE: c1920 charabanc outing; BELOW LEFT: scenic tours started in Water Street and RIGHT: the Allotment Gardeners' Assoc take a refresher in Lower Commercial Street, 1911.

Townsmen

John Dawson (1833-88) was a native of Settle, but from boyhood onward he was an inhabitant of Skipton, and attended the Grammar School. He was cashier at Dewhursts for 30 years, and proprietor of the *West Yorkshire Pioneer*. Admitted a member of the Skipton Congregational Church in 1853, he held a number of offices in the church — local preacher, deacon, secretary and Sunday School Superintendent.

One of his sons, William Harbutt Dawson, (1860-1948), was also educated at Skipton Grammar School, and began his researches into the history of his native town at the age of 18 years. *The History of Skipton* was published by Edmondson & Co in 1882; it was to be the first of over 20 books written by Harbutt Dawson, principally on Germany and its people.

In 1906 he left Skipton to take a Government appointment under Lloyd George, making a special study of social conditions in Germany, prior to the introduction of the first National Insurance Scheme in this country.

Of his many books, three were of local interest: the *History of Skipton* (1882), the *History of Independency in Skipton* (1891) and *Cromwell's Understudy* — a biography of Major-General John Lambert of Calton Hall in Kirkby Malhamdale. He married twice, each time to a German lady. His eldest son, William Siegfried Dawson, was Professor of Psychiatry at Sydney University. For his writings on Germany he was in 1936 awarded the honorary degree of PhD by the University of Koenigsburg.

Harbutt Dawson was not slow to voice his opinions about Skipton, curious as they sometimes are: 'It would be idle to speculate upon what the enterprise of the townspeople of Skipton may yet do. Many no doubt wish that it may some day bring about the removal of the one defect of the magnificent market-street, the blocks of buildings known as Middle Row. Perhaps the wish is a vain one'.

Walter Morrison (1836-1921) of Malham Tarn House was the fifth of seven sons and four daughters of James Morrison (1790-1857) of Morrison, Dillon and Co of Fore Street, London. Morrison worked his way up in the drapery business; his mother, Mary Ann was a daughter of John Todd of the same firm. His success depended on 'small profits and quick returns' and he made an immense fortune, a 'large part of which he expended in buying land in Berkshire, Buckinghamshire, Kent, Wiltshire, Yorkshire and Islay, Argyllshire'. On James Morrison's death in 1857, his English property was valued at between three and four million pounds, beside large investments in the USA.

Geoffrey Dawson (himself a Skiptonian and Editor of the *Times*) wrote Walter Morrison's obituary. 'Considering all his miscellaneous interests, an astonishing part of Morrison's time was spent at Malham Tarn, which had been acquired for him when he came of age from the Listers of Gisburn. Here he could indulge his love of walking, of folk-lore, of a very miscellaneous range of literature, and of local lordship in many forms. His notion of company was rather that of an audience than of a circle of friends. Visitors included Henry Fawcett, John Ruskin, Charles Darwin, John Stuart Hill, Sir William Harcourt and especially Charles Kingsley. It was at Malham Cove that Kingsley had the idea of the *Water Babies* and Walter Morrison was his "squire" '.

He was one of the founders of the Palestine Exploration Fund, and regarded himself in that capacity as the discoverer of Kitchener. In 1920 he gave a £50,000 endowment for the Bodleian Library at Oxford. The honorary DCL awarded to him 'was the only public recognition which he received, or indeed would have valued'.

On his death in 1921 his estate was sworn at two million pounds. C.J. Verity, later Chief General Manager of Martins Bank reminisced that one of his most vivid recollections was of the late Walter Morrison: 'several times a millionaire, his isolated country house was high on the moors of the Pennines at Malham Tarn about five miles from Settle. He had been chairman of the Craven Bank Ltd, was a governor of Giggleswick School to which he had given the most beautiful school chapel; a man of great stature, physically and otherwise, who showed an exquisite courtesy to us'. W.B. Carson (of the Bank) describes Walter Morrison, as 'the Craven multi-millionaire'. It is said that on returning from London to his home at Malham Tarn he would sometimes call in at Settle to buy a leg of mutton and carry it up to his home at Malham Tarn, a distance of several miles.

He was elected MP (Liberal) for Plymouth in 1861 and held that seat until the Liberal debacle in 1874, stood unsuccessfully for the City of London in 1880, parted with Mr Gladstone over his Irish programme, and twice successfully 1886-92 and 1895-1900 represented as a Liberal Unionist the Skipton division.

In 1874 he joined the board of the Central Argentine Railways, in which his family possessed a large stake, became its chairman in 1887 and his reports led to the absorption of the Buenos Aires and Rosario line. Educated at Eton and Balliol he became a redoubtable oar, and obtained a first class degree in lit. hum.

The pleasant Georgian house opposite the Parish Church, at the top of the High Street, was a private residence, and in 1867 Dr William Wylie moved from Settle to Skipton into this house — which is nos four and six High Street. In August 1878 Dr Wylie sold his practice and left for London where, according to the *Craven Pioneer* 'he has taken on a large and valuable practice'. He sold the Skipton practice to an Irishman, Dr John Forsythe Wilson (1850-1931) who, in August 1878 married Mary Jane Hanna. In 1882 his second son, Charles McMoran Wilson, was born at Skipton. In 1886, after Charles had had four attacks of rheumatic fever, Dr Forsythe Wilson moved south. Although Lord Moran (1882-1977) was only in Skipton for about four years of infancy, he could recall the Dewhurst family, who excelled at games, and Scotts the brewers, William Scott having married his aunt.

During the second world war, Charles (who had been knighted in 1938) accompanied Sir Winston Churchill as his personal physician on most of his wartime journeys. He wrote two books — *The Anatomy of Courage* (1945) and *Winston Churchill, the Struggle for Survival* (1966). Publication of the *Struggle for Survival* — Sir Charles' diaries chronicling the decline in Sir Winston's health — caused considerable controversy, and he was strongly criticised for publishing them.

In 1943 Sir Charles was elevated to the peerage under the title of Lord Moran. He died on 12 April 1977 at the age of 94. His eldest son and heir was Richard John McMoran Wilson.

It is curious that two of Skipton's most distinguished natives should be the sons of local doctors; Charles Wilson and the Rt Hon Iain Macleod, Chancellor of the Exchequer — born at Clifford House, Skipton.

On the front wall of Clifford House in Keighley Road appears a bronze plate, with the inscription as follows: 'Iain Norman Macleod, PC, MP, Chancellor of the Exchequer 1970, was born here on 11 November 1913. First elected to the House of Commons in 1950, he became Minister of Health in 1952, and later, served as Minister of Labour, Secretary of State for the Colonies, Chancellor of the Duchy of Lancaster and Leader of the House of Commons. He died at 11 Downing Street, London, on 20 July 1970'.

Iain Macleod was the son of Dr Norman Alex Macleod, who was in practice in Skipton for 30 years. He was baptised at Skipton Congregational Church. As a boy he attended St Monica's Convent kindergarten, and for a short time was a pupil of Ermysted's Grammar School, Skipton, before proceeding to Fettes College, Edinburgh.

Speaking at the Co-operative Hall on the occasion of the dinner in 1958 of the Grammar School Old Boys' Society, he congratulated the authorities who had discovered that he was an 'old boy'; he was not certain whether he was the only 'old boy of Ermysted's' to achieve cabinet office, but he was quite sure that he was the only old boy of St Monica's to do so.

The plaque mentioned above was unveiled by Lord Boyle, a former Conservative Minister of Education. Lord Boyle gave a short address: 'It is worthwhile spending a few minutes recalling the characteristics in Iain Macleod which everybody so admired. His wit, his combativeness, his ability to pack a punch at question time, were all devastating; but what engaged him most was policy-making, taking real decisions, participating at the centre of a governing party backed by a parliamentary majority. Iain was a great rhetorician. He could raise a party conference and nearly always commanded the House of Commons, something hard to do but vital for any government'.

Everyone remembered Iain Macleod's personal courage — his physical courage in the face of pain and discomfort, also his moral courage.

It was revealed that an Iain Macleod Trust Fund had been set up, and annual grants were to finance awards for educational purposes in schools and hospitals in the Craven district.

After Fettes, he went to Gonville and Caius College, Cambridge, where he took a BA in 1935. He played bridge for England at the age of 22, and published in 1952 *Bridge is an easy Game*. Joining the Army at the outbreak of war, in 1940 he gained a Commission and was wounded.

In 1946 he joined the Conservative Parliamentary Secretariat; in 1950 he was elected Conservative MP for Enfield West. In 1952 his career 'took off'. The reply he made to a speech on the National Health Charges Bill by the redoubtable Aneurin Bevan, impressed Churchill, who appointed him Minister of Health shortly afterwards. He was appointed Chancellor of the Exchequer when the Heath government took office in June 1970.

Skiptonians still remember a television broadcast which he planned in 1954, entitled 'Home Town' — the town being Skipton, and all the participants local people. In particular, shots were made of the two Skipton medical surgeries, and showed the successful working of medical partnerships.

The author's uncle, John Richard Barrow is third from the right in this study of the railwaymen of c1910.

OPPOSITE ABOVE: pest control in the early years of the century outside the New Ship Inn, and BELOW: sharing the spoils in polite society; ABOVE: on the right Henry Watson and next to him Mr Sloan — beating for the gentry's shoot? BELOW: The Amalgamated Society of Railway Servants gather on 28 June, 1908.

OPPOSITE ABOVE: Opening the new waterworks in July 1905 and BELOW: the Whit Monday walk when all denominations walked together — Catholics, then Christ Church, followed by the Parish Church and the combined chapels; ABOVE LEFT: Old Job Senior, the Rombalds Moor Hermit; CENTRE: Harriet Mellon (later Duchess of St Albans) who reputedly acted in Skipton; RIGHT: Peter Thornton, Town Crier in the late '20s; BELOW: Salvation Army Band, 1908.

ABOVE: Jack Guy (right) and his band; LEFT: Skipton Cricket Club: left to right — B. Crook, Reg Billows, T. Fleetwood, H.L. Thornton, S. Doughty; M. Windle, F. Homer, W. Greenwood, F. Furness, W. Bradley; A. Watson, C. Cooper and A. Holmes; RIGHT: Mr Manby emigrated to Kentucky, where he became a judge.

ABOVE: Among this between-wars group are Dick Walker, Howard Foster, Charlie Mathers, Mrs Foster, Miss Lizzie Storey, Miss Fanny Foster and Miss Beatrice Foster; BELOW: Frank Whalley believed in advertising.

95

ABOVE LEFT: George Smith drove Dr Liversidge's new motor; RIGHT: Manby's garage in Lower Union Street looked after the motoring pioneers; CENTRE: the doctor's house at the top (west) of High Street where John McMoran Wilson, later Lord Moran was born; BELOW LEFT: Dr N.A. Macleod, Iain Macleod's father, who practised in Skipton for many years, and CENTRE: Iain Macleod, (1913-1970) Chancellor of the Exchequer; (EB) RIGHT: Lord Moran (1882-1977), who was Winston Churchill's personal physician for many years. (MD)

Two Streets

Swadford Street is very old. Winterwell Hall (otherwise known as Lambert Hall) was there in 1449 when it was leased by Bolton Priory to William Malham, and in 1489 there is a reference to a 'burgage in Skipton in a street called Swatforth'.

Later usage, until about the middle of the last century, was for the street to be called 'Swadforth' — presumably the name derives from a former ford over Eller Beck.

In 1902, the *Craven Herald* records: 'Swadford Street, thanks to the railway, is rapidly changing in character from the quiet respectable family street it once was, to a busy mart of commerce'. In fact, development had started much earlier, with the arrival of the Leeds and Liverpool Canal in 1773.

Lambert Hall was originally known as Winterwell Hall, and Whitaker says it was so called probably from a well never frozen in winter, which is now swallowed up in the canal, and was more than half destroyed when that was cut.

R.B. Cragg (writing in the *Herald* in 1897) notes that 'Part of this Lambert Hall, otherwise Winterwell Hall was standing still within the memory of some of the older inhabitants, but then it had fallen from its lofty estate and only found shelter for the canal boatmen's horses, whilst the well from which it took its water was at the opposite side of the canal immediately in rear of the Conservative Club and was, until Skipton was supplied with water by the old waterworks company, one of the principal supplies for the inhabitants of Swadford Street and Union Square'.

When John Varley built Winterwell Buildings, he found the foundations of the old hall so immensely thick and sound, that he used them as foundations for the new structures. Whitaker says that Winterwell Hall was, about the middle of Henry VIII's reign, the residence of the Lamberts. It seems, he continues, not to have been without a degre of magnificence, for in an old rental it is described as containing the following apartments: 'the tower, the great parlour and chambers over it, the study chamber and parlour or study under it'.

The latest date we have for the Hall's occupation is 1665, when the Parish Register records the burial of 'Agnes, the daughter of Hugh Sawley, formerly of Marton, now liveth in a chamber at Lambert Hall in Skipton'.

Facing the Cock and Bottle and just across the street stands Swadforth House, not to be confused with Swadford House, now demolished, but formerly occupying the site of Burton's Buildings. R.B. Cragg, indulging his predilection for mixing fact with fiction says that the date of its erection was in the reign of King James II. By examining the rooms it will easily be seen why panelled rooms were looked upon with great suspicion both in Elizabeth's reign and during the Civil War, for doors, passages, and rooms for priests or others could easily be behind them.

Cragg mentions that four people could walk up the main staircase abreast, and adds 'There is a tradition that Cromwell's officers, including General Lambert, a Craven man, were quartered here for a time during the Civil War when Skipton Castle held out so obdurately for the King'. The house is advertised 'To Let' in 1815: 'This house is suitable for a large genteel family'.

In 1903 Mr G.W. Sloane the dentist opened a dental practice here. In 1928 the property was sold to the Skipton Industrial Co-operative Society Ltd. A new store was erected, and this is now swallowed up in Sunwin House.

Dr W.H. Dawson wrote in 1906: 'The Cock and Bottle Inn, a wayside inn of long ago in Swadford Street, is the only house in that street which has preserved anything of its old individuality. About fifty years ago the Cock and Bottle belonged to one Mr Smith. This gentleman made his will on a pewter pot — the why and wherefore can only be conjectured. The pot was afterwards stolen not, it is believed, by anyone who noticed the unusual use made of it, but for the value of the pewter. This pewter was traced as far as Leeds, but no further clue could be obtained, and when Mr Smith died his possessions went to the heir-at-law'.

The name 'Cock and Bottle' is respectably old; a deed of 1755 refers to a cottage in the Cock and Bottle Yard in Swadforth.

Newmarket Street is not one of the thoroughfares of Skipton on whose past the inhabitants are inclined to dwell with nostalgic affection. The century up to 1939 saw this neighbourhood deteriorate from a first-class residential area to a street where, in the words of a writer in the *Craven Herald* in 1927 'it is a trifle squalid, very dull, and much too long. The houses are huddled and of all shapes and sizes: the causeway is on a few different planes (even cobbles); the chimney pots are of amazing diversity. Nobody who'd ever heard of the fascinating subject of town planning would have allowed its buildings to be bundled together so fancifully and so irresponsibly. Newmarket Street is a hotch-potch that looks unappetising in the broth pan, but is very palatable in spoonfuls'.

This street was the line of the old road to Ilkley and York, leading up Shode Bank (Short Bank Road) and over Rombalds Moor. The low road through Draughton was not opened until 1803. It was known as 'the Newmarket' as early as 1555, possibly to distinguish it from the older market in the Market Place (the lower half of High Street) but it was not, as Dawson suggests, the Corn Market: this was in the upper part of High Street, near the Public Library.

The 'hotchpotch' of 1927 is now in course of transformation into a neat, orderly development. Of the gentlemen's residences in the old street only a handful remain. Two of them were the houses of 19th century solicitors: that of John Preston and his son Thomas Baynes Preston is now a dental surgery, and Phillips shop was erected by John Carr, and later became the residence in turn of Dr Macnab, Dr Wylie, Dr Readman, Dr Kitching and Dr W.H. Robinson. The third, which has since 1926 housed the British Legion Club, was in the middle of the last century the home of Dr William Birtwhistle.

The street also retains the row of old shops on the south side leading out of Caroline Square, and Devonshire Terrace, erected about 1814. Only one old inn survives from the 18th century: the Devonshire Hotel, built in the 1780s by the Duke of Devonshire as the 'New Inn', and more recently two further old inns have lost their licences. The Craven Arms, formerly the Craven Vaults, was a spirit merchant's shop but is now an estate agents' office. The Hart's Head, formerly a thatched cottage, is now a boutique and Messrs Ashe and Nephew's wineshop.

The Nag's Head has vanished: this house featured in Baines' 1822 *Directory* and lost its licence in 1909. It subsequently served as a fish and chip shop — the Nags Head Fishery — before being demolished in 1966. The Cross Keys has moved from Tradesmen's Place to the Old Grammar School. Tradesmen's Place with Club Houses at the rear, were built early in the last century by the Tradesmen's Sick Club.

Club Houses have vanished, along with Miss Brown's Yard, Petty's Court and Greenside, all on the south side of Newmarket Street, and Carr's Yard, Brown's Yard and Bartle Holmes' Yard on its north side. Only Hardcastle's Ginnel (normally called merely the latter, leading to the Friends' Meeting House of 1693) and Brookside (formerly Quaker's Place) remain.

Of the substantial houses which have gone, the best known was Dyneley House, once the home (from 1851 to 1866) of John Bonny Dewhurst, and then until 1884 of Col George Robinson, general manager of the Craven Bank: here in 1871 was born George Geoffrey Robinson, who later adopted the surname of Dawson and became Editor of *The Times*. A surgery was recently built on the old site of the Dyneley.

Newmarket House — which Skiptonians will remember better as Conways Model Lodging House — was a 'new erected mansion' in 1805, and became the home of Dr Richard Smith and later of John Dawson, Editor of the *Craven Pioneer,* who moved here from the newly built Crete House, now Messrs T.H. Taylor and Son's offices, which owes more to being built in concrete than to any exotic Mediterranean associations.

Stanley House, demolished to make way for the Telephone Exchange, was a six-bedroomed house, occupied for years by James Brown and his spinster daughters Isabel, Grace and Jane.

The Congregational Chapel was built in 1778 and rebuilt in 1838; the Sunday School in 1891.

At the far end of the street were the Parish Clerk's house (No 83) and the Bar House for the old highway over Rombalds Moor, and home of the Parish Constable (No 85). Beyond them was the Grammar School, founded by William Ermysted in 1548, which did not move to Gargrave Road until 1876.

While, therefore, we recall the early 19th century glories of this ancient street, let us also remember that during the present century these glories had distinctly faded. Most of the buildings had become dingy and unattractive, and no tears need be shed about their passing. Certainly, Newmarket Street in 1983 is a more pleasant street to live in, and to shop in, then it was up to a few years ago.

Billy Gellin must have been the best known character in Skipton, with his waistcoat (no shirt) and his hand-cart for scavenging coal from the Leeds and Liverpool Canal. The mill-owners always arranged to 'spill' sufficient coal for Billy's needs. He was also dignified with a top hat — worn on Sundays only.

The junction of the two streets — Caroline Square, where Woolworth's
is now.

OPPOSITE ABOVE: Swadford Street, showing the Cock and Bottle on the left and Swadforth House on the right; LEFT: old Dr Fisher's house in Swadford Street; RIGHT: Ship Hotel, rebuilt c1889 and closed in 1924, and BELOW: part of the Ship Hotel fronting Caroline Square c1885; Christ Church Vicarage can be seen in the distance; ABOVE LEFT: previous Co-op store before the new Sunwin House was built; CENTRE: Swadford Street from Ship Corner to Belmont Bridge c1907, and ABOVE RIGHT: testing Pinder Bridge, 9 November 1910; BELOW LEFT: Sackville Street c1905, and RIGHT: the Old Unicorn and Baldwin's Fold on the present site of the Regal cinema.

ABOVE LEFT: Old Unicorn Hotel, demolished for road widening and rebuilt about 1923; RIGHT: Swadford House, home of James Hargreaves the dentist, demolished 1936; CENTRE: stepping stones across Wilderness Beck; this area is now culverted; BELOW LEFT: a pleasant Georgian House, Newmarket Street, now a dental surgery, and RIGHT: Newmarket Street, Frearson, now part of the new YEB shop; Skipton Building Society occupied the adjoining building on the right.

ABOVE: Newmarket Street, north side; the large three storey house was Stanley House, demolished to make way for the new telephone exchange, and BELOW: Newmarket Street houses demolished in 1966.

LEFT: Nags Head, which lost its licence in 1909 and became the Nag's Head Fisheries; BELOW: Billy Gellin stands with his barrow at the end of Newmarket Street, and RIGHT: Club Houses off Newmarket Street, demolished 1958.

ABOVE: The whole of this south side of Newmarket Street has disappeared, and LEFT: the three storey building known as Newmarket House finished its days as a model lodging house; RIGHT: Birtwistle's yard off the High Street end of Newmarket Street, now gone.

ABOVE: Greenside, a yard off Newmarket Street, now part of Petyt Grove, and BELOW: Craven Arms lost its licence in 1974.

The Fourth Estate

Skipton's first periodical was the *Skipton Advertiser and Monthly Recorder,* printed and published by John Garnett, the first number of which was issued in December 1852, declaring that its object was 'to advocate the principles of morality, social science, commerce and agriculture, and to promote the best interests of the town and district'. At first, an editorial committee contributed and controlled the contents of this 8-page periodical but, as this disintegrated, Garnett ill-advisedly allowed the insertion of a matrimonial column setting forth the qualifications, mental and otherwise, of eligible young ladies, whose initials were added so that there could be little doubt as to their identity. Enraged spinsters and their indignant mothers raised a storm of protest, in which the *Advertiser* foundered. Garnett sold his business and left the town in January 1856.

One month after the birth of the *Advertiser* came, in January 1853, the first issue of the monthly journal, the *Craven Herald,* price one penny, printed by John Tasker & Son at 31 High Street, Skipton. This was brought before the public as a 'Journal of Literature and Science'. In January 1858, James Tasker, who had succeeded to the business, was appointed Postmaster at Skipton, an office which prevented him from publishing a newspaper, and the first *Craven Herald* ceased.

In August 1854 the Skipton Temperance Society, an influential and energetic body, issued a free tract-journal, the *Home Visitor,* which can only by a stretch of imagination be described as a newspaper. It was edited by the indefatigable John Dawson, who, to quote his son Dr W. Harbutt Dawson, was 'then an eager young man who had attracted attention by his active interest in public affairs, and particularly in moral and religious movements'. In 1856 Robert Tasker took over John Garnett's printing business, and arranged to print the *Home Visitor and Advertiser* whose motto was 'the promotion of home happiness and the public good'. Still under the patronage of the Skipton Temperance Society, and the editorship of John Dawson, the periodical became, in April 1858, the *Skipton Pioneer and Craven Chronicle and Advertiser.*

In April 1859, the *Craven Pioneer and Skipton Home Advertiser* became a fortnightly newspaper and passed entirely into the hands of John Dawson. From January 1861 the *Craven Weekly Pioneer and General Advertiser* was published weekly, beginning with a circulation of 800. Robert Tasker (who had been apprenticed to his father's cousin John Tasker) continued as printer until December 1865, when Edmondson & Co took over, this firm being constituted by Thomas Edmondson, a practical printer, and financed by John Dawson, a sleeping partner.

In the meantime, the passing of the original *Craven Herald* had left the town with only one newspaper, and another Skipton printer, John Procter Brown, tried to fill the gap with the *Skipton Reporter* which lasted only from February 1858 to September 1860, when it was sold to J.C. Cragg, a Keighley printer, who continued it fortnightly for a short time, but without success.

The Local Board of Health, the forerunner of the Urban District Council, was formed in 1858, and public awareness of political issues increased. The Dawson family was staunchly nonconformist and Liberal, and throughout the sixties the *Pioneer* had a monopoly. As early as April 1872, a meeting of Conservatives held at the Town Hall, recommended that efforts be made to establish in Skipton a weekly newspaper in the Conservative interest. This led to the incorporation of the Craven

Conservative Newspaper Co Ltd, which on 10 July 1874 altered its name to the Skipton Stationery Co Ltd, and a week later purchased the leasehold property and printing and stationery business of the retiring James Tasker, at 38 High Street. Here they revived the name of Tasker's earlier newspaper, the *Craven Herald,* and on 24 October 1874 began over a century of uninterrupted publication of a still flourishing local newspaper.

John Dawson, the owner-editor of the *Pioneer,* died in 1880, and the editorship passed to his son William Harbutt Dawson (1860-1948) who had already in 1882 published his *History of Skipton.*

To quote Dr Dawson again 'On his initiative, the title had already been changed to the *West Yorkshire Pioneer* in order to conform with the increasing range of its influence, and thereafter the journal enjoyed a long and unbroken run of popularity. During this second and younger editorship, greater emphasis was given in this journal's columns to social and political questions, and it became recognised more and more as an independent adviser to the local Liberal party'. Early in 1905, Harbutt Dawson took up a government appointment under Lloyd George, making a special study of social conditions in Germany preparatory to the introduction of a National Health Insurance Scheme in this country. The *Pioneer* was sold to the Liberal party, and then to a northern newspaper combine, which in turn, sold the goodwill and title to the *Craven Herald* in 1937. Since this date we have had the *Craven Herald and Pioneer.*

The Yorkshire Dales District Railway opening of Grassington Station.

Building the YD Railway.

HOME  VISITOR,

AND SKIPTON ADVERTISER,

CONDUCTED BY THE COMMITTEE OF THE SKIPTON TEMPERANCE SOCIETY.

VOL. I.—No. 1.] APRIL, 1856. 1,000 Copies, [ONE HALF-PENNY EACH.

R. TASKER,
(Late Garnett,)

PRINTER, STATIONER, & BOOKBINDER,

BEGS most respectfully to inform the Inhabitants of SKIPTON and the Neighbourhood, that he has purchased the whole of the STOCK-IN-TRADE and Good-will in the Shop and Premises lately occupied by Mr. John Garnett, in the continuance of whose business he hopes, by Personal Attention and Moderate Charges, to merit a share of public patronage and support.

R. T. begs to call attention to his STOCK of BOOKS, which contains a choice selection of Popular and Modern Works. Also, a large Stock of Ledgers, Day Books, Memorandums, Copy Books, and School Books of every description. A well-assorted and fashionable stock of STATIONERY always on hand.

Engraving, Lithography, and Letter Press Printing, executed on the Shortest Notice, and in the best Style of Workmanship. Circulars, Bill Heads, Address Cards, Drawings, Plans, &c., neatly executed to order.

London and Provincial Newspapers may be had either at the Shop or direct by Post.

AGENT FOR THE

UNITED SERVICE AND GENERAL
LIFE ASSURANCE GUARANTEE ASSOCIATION,
LONDON.

Empowered by Royal Letters Patent.

☞ PUNCTUALITY, *in the execution of all Orders, may be strictly relied upon.*

MRS. S. COOKE,

BEGS most respectfully to inform the Ladies of Skipton and its Neighbourhood, that she Cleans CARPETS, HEARTH-RUGS, DRUGGETS, &c., in Superior Style; and hopes, by strict attention, to merit their favours.

Residence—UNION SQUARE, SKIPTON.

JUST PUBLISHED,

A Series of New REWARD BOOKS, at ONE HALFPENNY each; amongst which are Descriptive DIALOGUES on the NATIVITY: the CRUCIFIXION: the RESURRECTION: and the ASCENSION: each to be recited by SIX GIRLS;

By B. BAILEY, Skipton.

Also, by the same Author,

The Pearls of Craven:

Descriptive of the Scenery in that District; with numerous Engravings. Price—

Handsomely Bound .... 1s. 6d.

The Gems of Wharfedale:
Ilkley, Bolton and the Neighbourhood; with Engravings, Price 6d., and a Guide up the

North Western:
Settle, Hornby, Lancaster, Morecambe and the vicinity—with Engravings. Price 6d.

The Eleventh Edition of 36,000
OF THE
Infantile Class Book:
Price to Schools, 3s. 6d. per doz. The Second Edition of
The Pictorial Reading Book:
Price to Schools, 3s. 6d.

The Pig:
How to Breed and how to Feed; 20 Engravings,—Price only 3d.

Shortly will be published,

Harrison's Juvenile Expositor,
For the use of Schools; Price (bound) only 6d.

☞ Sold Wholesale by the Publishers, J. Harrison and Son, Courant Office, Bingley, and may be had of Messrs. Robert Tasker, and John Winterbottom, Skipton.

CARLTON-IN-CRAVEN

TO BE LET,

With Immediate Possession, a well-built and comfortable

COTTAGE,

Suitable for a single Lady or Gentleman, or a Married Couple without family. RENT reasonable.

☞ Apply to Mr. S. THOMPSON, Post Office, Carlton.

ABOVE: *The Home Visitor* of April 1856; OPPOSITE LEFT: *The Craven Herald* of November 1853; RIGHT: Ranger's *Report* on sanitary conditions in Skipton 1857, and BELOW: *The Craven Pioneer* office in Lower Middle Row 1875.

110

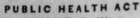

PUBLIC HEALTH ACT
(11 & 12 Vict. Cap. 63.)

REPORT

TO THE

GENERAL BOARD OF HEALTH

ON A

PRELIMINARY INQUIRY

INTO THE SEWERAGE, DRAINAGE, SUPPLY OF
WATER, AND THE SANITARY CONDITION
OF THE INHABITANTS

OF THE TOWNSHIP OF

SKIPTON,

IN THE WEST RIDING OF THE COUNTY OF YORK.

BY WILLIAM RANGER, Esq. C.E.

SUPERINTENDING INSPECTOR.

LONDON:
PRINTED BY GEORGE E. EYRE AND WILLIAM SPOTTISWOODE,
PRINTERS TO THE QUEEN'S MOST EXCELLENT MAJESTY.
FOR HER MAJESTY'S STATIONERY OFFICE.

1857.

THE
Craven Agricultural Society.

›››◦‹‹‹

A CATALOGUE

OF THE

CATTLE, HORSES, SHEEP, PIGS, POULTRY, ROOTS, IMPLEMENTS, &c., &c.

EXHIBITED AT THE

FIFTH ANNUAL MEETING

OF THE SOCIETY,

HELD AT SKIPTON,

On Friday, the 16th of September, 1859.

SKIPTON:
PRINTED BY ROBERT TASKER, MARKET-PLACE.
MDCCCLIX.

Craven Agricultural Show catalogue of 1859.

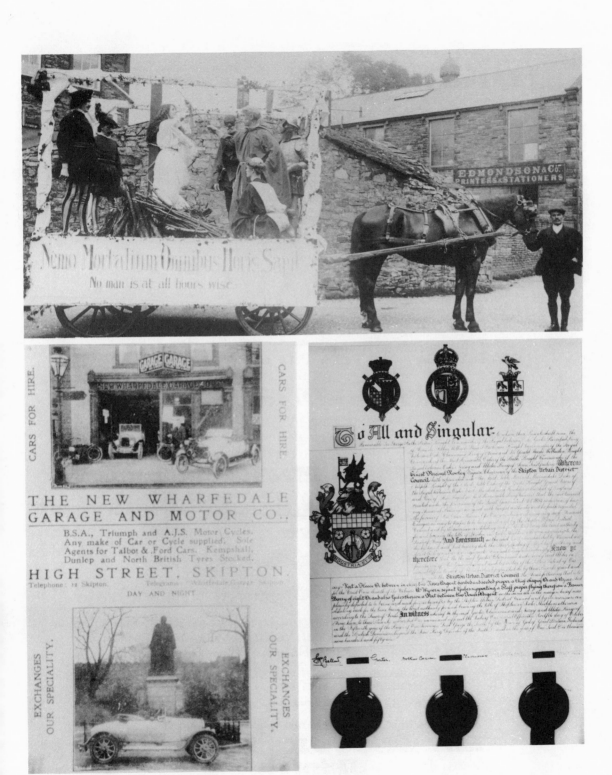

ABOVE: Skipton Hospital Gala float near Edmondson & Co (printers of *The Craven Herald*); LEFT: advertising poster of the New Wharfedale Garage and Motor Co; (note the price of the car); RIGHT: Skipton UDC's Grant of Arms of 1951, when Ernest Percival Rowley (the author's father) was Chairman.

Skipton in Craven.

Dwelling House
AND SHOP.

TO BE

Sold by Auction,

By Mr. Merryweather,

On Saturday the 18th Day of November, 1826,

AT THE

Black-Horse-Hotel, in Skipton,

BETWIXT THE HOURS OF SIX AND EIGHT O'CLOCK IN THE EVENING,

Subject to such Conditions as will be then and there produced;

ALL THAT

Leasehold Messuage, or

DWELLING HOUSE
AND
SHOP.

MOST abvantageously situated in the **MIDDLE ROW**, in Skipton, now in the possession of Mr. DENBIGH, Ironmonger, the Shop having been for some time occupied in that Line of Business.

The Premises are held under Lease from the EARL of THANET, at the Yearly Ground Rent of Two Guineas; and Thirty-Eight Years of the Term are now unexpired.

For further Particulars enquire at the Office of

Mr. ALCOCK, Solicitor, Skipton.

PRINTED BY JOHN GARNETT, BOOKSELLER, STATIONER, & BOOKBINDER, SKIPTON.

A Middle Row lease goes under the hammer in 1826.

SALE OF VALUABLE
Freehold Premises,
IN SKIPTON,
DUTY FREE.

To be Sold by Auction,
BY JOHN GARNETT,

By order of the Assignees, of the real and Personal Estate, of Mr. WILLIAM YOUNG, a Bankrupt

At the Black Horse Inn, in Skipton,
On TUESDAY the 17th Day of NOVEMBER, 1840,

At SIX o'Clock in the Evening precisely, subject to such Conditions as will be then and there produced:—

ALL THAT

VALUABLE FREEHOLD
Messuage,
Dwelling-House,
AND SHOP,

Situate in a commanding situation, in the centre of the Market-Place,

in the Town of Skipton aforesaid; now or late in the occupation of the said *Wm. Young*, together with a good **BACK KITCHEN** and **BREWERY**, thereto adjoining and belonging.

Also all those good and commodious BUILDINGS and PREMISES,

Situate up the Yard, behind the above mentioned Premises; consisting of **THREE EXCELLENT COTTAGES**, two of them being in the several occupations of *Jno. Astin*, and *Wm. Redieough*, and the remaining one unoccupied. Together with the **GARDEN** and **CONVENIENCES**, thereto adjoining and belonging. Also all that **PIG STYE** and **GRANARY**, over the same; and all that **BARN** at the extremity of the Garden, adjoining upon and opening into the Back Lane, in the Town of Skipton aforesaid.

⁎⁎ *The above Premises are exceedingly well situated for the purposes of Trade, and afford a good Opportunity for profitable Investment, by an enterprising Tradesman.*

☞ **For further Particulars apply at the Offices of**

Mr. ALCOCK, in Skipton,
THE SOLICITOR TO THE ASSIGNEES.

J. GARNETT, PRINTER, BOOKBINDER, &c., MARKET-PLACE, SKIPTON.

An 1840 Market Place property comes up for sale.

SKIPTON.

SALE OF
Valuable Leasehold Property.

To be Sold by Auction,

BY MR. JOHN GARNETT,

At the BLACK HORSE HOTEL, in SKIPTON,

IN THE COUNTY OF YORK;

On Wednesday the 11th day of September, 1844,

COMMENCING AT SIX O'CLOCK IN THE AFTERNOON PRECISELY,

EITHER ALTOGETHER OR IN THE FOLLOWING OR SUCH OTHER LOTS AS MAY BE DETERMINED ON AT THE TIME OF THE SALE;

THE FOLLOWING

LEASEHOLD HOUSES,
SHOPS, WAREHOUSES, AND IRON FOUNDRY,

THAT IS TO SAY:----

Lot 1. ALL that Messuage or Dwellinghouse and Warehouses, and Shop, with the Yards, Outbuildings and Appurtenances thereto belonging, situate in Skipton aforesaid, adjoining the Leeds and Liverpool Canal and in the Occupation of Mr. EDWARD ROBINSON.

Also all those Five Messuages, Cottages, or Dwellinghouses, adjoining the lastly described Premises, now or lately in the several Tenures or Occupations of JOHN SMITH, (Wagoner;) RICHARD COWMAN, WILLIAM WADE, MARY FELL, and JOHN SMITH, (Boatman.)

Lot 1 is held for the remainder of a Term of Forty Years, which will expire on the 12th of May, 1852, under the Yearly Ground Rent of £2. 2s. 0d. payable half-yearly.

The Premises in the Occupation of Mr. EDWARD ROBINSON, are demised to him for a Term of Seven Years, which will expire on the 1st Day of November, 1847, under the Yearly Rent of £80, payable half-yearly on the 1st Day of April and the 1st Day of October, and will be offered for Sale subject to such Lease.

Lot 2. ALL that Messuage or Dwellinghouse and Shop, situate in Caro-line Square, in the Town of Skipton aforesaid, in the Occupation of Mrs. WILSON.

Lot 2 is held for the remainder of a Term of Fifty Years, which will expire on the 12th of May, 1864, under the Yearly Ground Rent of £2. 2s. payable half-yearly.

Lot 3. ALL that spacious and very convenient Iron Foundry, with the Messuage or Dwellinghouse, and the Work-Shop, Stable, Warehouse, and Premises thereto belonging, in the Occupation of Mrs. WILSON, situate in Skipton aforesaid, and adjoining the Gas Works and the said Canal.

Lot 3 is held for the remainder of a Term of Thirty Years, which will expire on the 8th of September, 1858, under the Yearly Rent of £1. 10s. payable half-yearly.

Lot 4. The Tenant Right of all that Garden, in the Occupation of WILLIAM CARR, lying along the Road leading from Skipton to Kildwick, and situate at a short distance from the Premises consisting of Lot 1.

Lot 4 is subject to a Rent of 2s. payable half-yearly.

Lot 5. SIX SHARES IN THE SKIPTON GAS-WORKS.

•.• All the above BUILDINGS have been put into a complete state of Repair. Lots 1 and 3, being on the Bank of the Canal, running close by the Town, and Lot 2, being in the heart of the important Town of Skipton, are admirably situated for carrying on extensive Trades to great advantage, and the whole Property presents a very favorable opportunity for Investment.

For further information apply to Mr. WILLIAM HOWSON, of Settle; Mr. ISAAC DEWHURST, of Skipton; or at the Offices of

SKIPTON, 15th AUGUST, 1844.

Mr. ALCOCK, Solicitor, Skipton.

PRINTED BY J. GARNETT, BOOKSELLER, &c. MARKET-PLACE, SKIPTON.

Leydon's Trust sells a parcel of leasehold properties in 1844.

116

Damp and Detention

In November 1914, Bradford Corporation erected a camp at the top of what is now Salisbury Street to accommodate men of the 'Bradford Pals Regiment'. The site lay between the Hollow at the Girl's High School and the houses in Raikes Road. Few who participated in the march from Bradford to Skipton during the drenching rain, early in 1915, are likely to forget the sight of the camp on their arrival. It was in a rough state, but the 'Pals' quickly settled down, and the hutments soon assumed an aspect of comfort, which was in itself evidence of good order and discipline. The 'Pals' were perhaps the most popular of the battalions which occupied the huts and it was with genuine regret that the townspeople watched them march away some months later.

After the 'Pals' departed a number of other regiments occupied the camp until finally in January 1918 German POWs, 546 officers and 137 men, arrived and were accommodated in the camp.

One German's comment on the weather is interesting — there is little sunshine, the cloud cover which normally enveloped him very dark and inhospitable. 'It rained and rained without stopping'.

With the Armistice in 1918 the guards were withdrawn and the prisoners put on their honour not to escape. They left on 24 October 1919.

At the subsequent sale of equipment, including 2,000 army blankets and 39 men's sleeping huts at £117 10s 0d each, Bradford Corporation was the largest purchaser. The YMCA hut was sold privately to the Bradford Branch of the Comrades of the Great War. Twelve sentry boxes and sentry gantries came under the hammer; six ex-army huts are still to be found in and about Skipton and three huts were in use at the Grammar School until 1932, (the Top hut, the Middle hut and the Bottom hut.) It is likely that three further huts were sold, which now form part of Embsay Institute, Angus's Garage and Wm Lawson & Sons timber store, off Sackville Street.

The Raikeswood Camp should not be confused with Overdale Camp, which is now the site of the Overdale Trailer Park. Overdale Camp was throughout the last war a POW camp, housing first the Italians and then the Germans.

'The Flood' in Skipton was commonly all that was necessary to identify the flood of 3 June 1908, and numerous postcard pictures of the events were issued, showing the devastation at Waterfall Ghyll, damage to Millholme Shed at Embsay, and the bursting of the Long Dam and the Round Dam in the Castle Woods. The cause of the flood was a torrential storm on Rylstone Fell. Eller Beck smashed through Skipton Woods, carrying with it bridges, stones and debris; the Round Dam collapsed and water flooded out in a foaming waterfall, the towing path of Springs Canal being in some places two or three feet under water. Canal Wharf, off Belmont Bridge was flooded.

In June 1979 another disastrous flood occurred. One and a quarter inches of rain fell on Skipton over the lunch time period on Wednesday 13 June in two violent storms.

Water ran straight off the land into already swollen streams and a flood of water, carrying mud and debris, came down Wilderness and Skibeden Becks into Waller Hill Beck. The Swadford Street-Keighley Road area of the town was flooded to over six feet deep and one old lady living in Brookside was unfortunately drowned. The old peoples' bungalows were badly affected and in Dewhurst's mill looms and electrical equipment were completely submerged.

On Sunday 6 June 1982 two hours of torrential rain again left the centre of Skipton under five feet of muddy water, in a replica of the disastrous flood of three years ago. Water poured into the town centre like a tidal wave. Shopkeepers who had been told that it could only happen once in every hundred years provoked the dry remark that 'it has been a very short hundred years'. A notice on Cavendish-Woodhouse's window said, 'CLOSED TODAY — NEXT HIGH TIDE 12.00 pm'. More than an inch of water fell in Skipton in under three hours, slightly less than in the 1976 flood.

A German prisoner's view of the Parish Church tower.

ABOVE: Lagerstrasse (Camp Street) in Raikeswood POW Camp;
BELOW: the Camp.

119

Clearing out the Leeds and Liverpool Canal after the flood.

ABOVE: Trouble at the Eller Beck/Springs Canal in June, 1908 and
BELOW: more trouble.

ABOVE: The Round Dam in Skipton, Castle Woods; LEFT: water pouring from the canal in the 1908 flood, and RIGHT: the flood in the Dock Yard; BELOW: the overflow from the canal near Belmont Bridge in the 1908 flood.

ABOVE: The flood in Skipton Woods 1908, and BELOW: Springs canal
after the flood.

ABOVE: The flood in 1979, looking towards Ship Corner from Swadford Street, and BELOW: looking from Ship Corner up Keighley Road.

Victorian Town

Queen Victoria succeeded to the throne on 20 June 1837. The first foundation stone of a new Parish Church in Craven was laid at Christ Church, Skipton, on 21 June 1837. The crowd joined vociferously in the chorus of *God Save the King*; the news of the death of King William IV had not yet reached the town.

The truth is that Skipton in 1837 was at a low ebb. The precipitous Shode Bank had been replaced by the Toll Road to Draughton as the main highway to York, and the 'New Line' (Gargrave Road) had just been constructed, but Skipton was still little more than a large country village.

The Castle, which should have injected life and prosperity into the community, was owned by the 11th and last Earl of Thanet, who lived in Kent, leaving his Craven estates to the care of a steward; the Parish Church was superintended by a Vicar, Reverend John Pering, who lived at Kildwick and left the souls at Skipton in the charge of a curate. There had been no resident Vicar at Skipton since Reverend John Parry MA went mad in 1778. The ancient Grammar School was 'very old, ill-ventilated and lighted, and of insufficient size', and ambitious Skiptonians sent their sons to Carleton School, which had a better reputation. The Headmaster at Skipton was the ailing Reverend William Sidgwick, who is better known for his connections — his father was proprietor of the town's first cotton spinning mill, the High Mill, opened in 1785 at the entrance to Skipton Woods; his daughter Minnie married the Archbishop of Canterbury, and his brother John Benson Sidgwick was in 1839 to employ one Charlotte Brontë as a rather unsatisfactory governess to his children.

The absentee Lords of the Honour of Skipton were criticised by Frederick Montagu, in his *Gleanings in Craven* in 1838: 'It is true, if an ancient building yields to time's calls, and crumbles to the earth, a new building is essential, because crumbs yield no rent. This is the only local improvement that is ever made; it will always be found, that monopoly has one son called indifference, who has had the cramp during the whole of his life'.

Montagu goes on to applaud the enterprise of Dr Thomas Dodgson, who considered a sulphur spring in Short Bank Road to be of great medicinal value, and who founded Skipton Baths at great expense. Unhappily, the doctor's initiative was disastrously rewarded. This popular physician, who had commenced practice in the town in 1822, was the author in 1832 of *A Practical Essay on casual and habitual Intemperance*. Impoverished by the failure of the Baths project, he himself succumbed to drink, and is said to have died in the workhouse in 1866.

In 1837 the Market Cross still stood in the Market Place, the very name of which has now lapsed. The Clerks of the Market were required to take an oath: 'that you shall well and truly serve our Sovereign Lady the Queen and the Lord of this Leet in the offices of Ale Tasters and Clerks of the Market for this Manor . . . you shall duly and true see that the Bread Beer and Ale within your liberty be good and wholesome; you shall make diligent search each market day and oftener that no person or persons sell bad or corrupt flesh butter or other victualling whatsoever, and that no person or persons use deceipt in their trade or buy or sell by short or false weights or measures'.

The Fair was last proclaimed at Skipton in 1856 — at the same time as the proclamation of peace after the Crimean War. The manorial officers vanished, superseded by the Local Board of Health, then the Urban District Council, and now the Craven District Council with the Skipton Town Council.

Many of the inns at which the ale-tasters plied their trade have also disappeared. Since Victoria died in 1901, no less than 14 inns in the town have closed — The Fountain, Old George, Thanet's Arms, Wheatsheaf, Hole-in-the-Wall and King's Arms (all six in the Main Street); the Nag's Head, Hart's Head and Craven Arms (in Newmarket Street); the Joiner's Arms in Lower Commercial Street, William IV in Water Street, and the Star Inn in Keighley Road, the Ship Hotel on Ship Corner and the New Ship on Mill Bridge.

What was life like in Skipton when Victoria came to the throne? A Mrs Brown (born 1823) was interviewed by the *Craven Herald* in 1913: horses in those days were changed at Kendal, Settle, Skipton and Keighley on the way south. Speaking of her life as a girl, Mrs Brown said that at that time Skipton possessed but one constable, his name was Tom Lowcock, and his method of dealing with prisoners was distinctly unique. The official 'Police Station' was in a room in the basement of the then Mechanics' Institute — now the Friendly Societies Hall — and often Tom used to consider this apartment a somewhat unwholesome place for the housing of offenders. Occasionally his sympathy for his charge took a practical turn, and he conveyed him to his private residence in Chancery Lane, where he handcuffed him securely to the oven door. For a number of years Constable Lowcock discharged his onerous duties single-handed and, although he was at one time joined by a colleague named Whittingham, the latter did not remain long in the town Mrs Brown described Lowcock as a 'terror' who, despite the comparatively heavy duties of his office, managed to preserve, as a rule, a fair measure of law and order.

At about 15 years of age she learned to weave at Messrs Sidgwick's factory — High Mill. At that time children commenced work at 8 years of age; any boy or girl who was at all active and healthy was sent to the mill, where work was carried on from 6 in the morning until 8 at night. An operative managing three looms could earn as much as 15 shillings per week.

During Victoria's long reign the town ceased to be a withdrawn, enclosed community, and was opened up as the 'Gateway to the Dales', when the railways arrived. The Bradford line came first in 1847, followed by a line into North Lancashire in 1848, to Lancaster in 1849 and to Ilkley in 1888. When Victoria died in 1901 the line to Grassington was under construction, but the railways were already doomed.

Skipton owed its position as an ancient market town to its strategic situation at the junction of highways from Leeds to Carlisle, and from York to Lancaster. The industrial revolution, heralded by the arrival of the canal in 1773, more than doubled the town's population between 1801 and 1841. The railways brought further growth to the town — from 5,000 to 12,000 during the Victorian era — but the services of an agricultural market town remained, and the cattle market continued to be held in the streets until 1906.

The Queen's Diamond Jubilee in 1897 was a final demonstration of the glories of the British Empire, but progress was reaching country districts and, in the following year, the Jubilee Procession in London could be seen in animated pictures in Skipton Town Hall. 1897 also saw an omen of change which was radically to affect the town: the first motor car passed through High Street that year.

Cottages, High Mill, Skipton Woods.

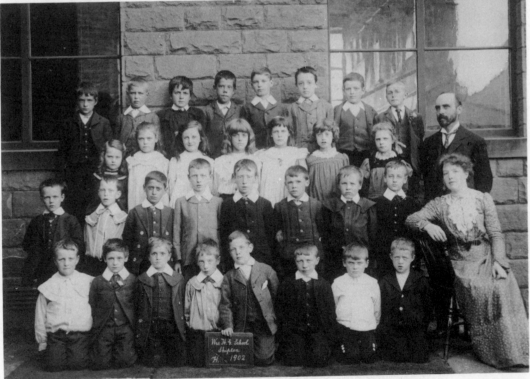

ABOVE: 21 June 1887, and the gentlemen of the town gather in Brick Hall Yard to inspect the 'whole roasted ox' on the hoof for Queen Victoria's Jubilee celebrations; BELOW: the Wesleyan H.G. School — class of 1902.

RULES

FOR THE

SKIPTON WESLEYAN SUNDAY SCHOOL.

1850.

THE COMMITTEE.

1. THE Committee shall consist of the Ministers stationed in the Circuit, the Superintendents, the Treasurer, and Secretary, the Librarian, and 10 of the Teachers, seven of whom (including a Chairman) shall constitute a quorum.

2. The Superintendent Minister of the Circuit, (or, in his absence, his Colleague) shall be Chairman of all the meetings of the Committee he may attend, but, in his absence, the members present shall elect a Chairman out of their own number.

3. Five of the Committee shall retire annually, and shall be eligible for re-election, and their places be supplied by the Annual Teachers' Meeting.

4. The Committee shall fill up any vacancies in their number occurring in the course of the year.

5. The sole control and management of the School, the selection and appointment of Teachers and Officers, and expulsion of Scholars, (subject to the regulations hereinafter mentioned) shall be vested in the Committee, who shall meet monthly to attend to its affairs.

6. In moving Teachers from lower to higher classes, special care shall be taken to select those who give the best proofs of decided piety, ability, punctuality and diligence.

7. A special Committee meeting may be held on a request being made to the Secretary, signed by three of the members of the Committee.

THE TREASURER.

1. THE Treasurer shall receive all monies, and meet all demands on behalf of the School, under the direction of the Committee.

2. He shall present the accounts of the School for the year, to be audited by the Committee, at their meeting in January in every year.

THE SECRETARY.

1. THE Secretary must call all the Meetings of the Committee or Teachers at the times appointed; he must attend the same, and enter correctly their proceedings in the Secretary's Minute Book.

ANNUAL TEACHERS' MEETING.

1. A Meeting of the Teachers shall be held in the month of November or December in each year, for the purpose of selecting the Superintendents and Committee, and a Minister to preach the Anniversary Sermons.

2. The Committee shall furnish lists of Persons nominated by them, containing twice the number to be elected as members of the Committee and Superintendents, out of which the Meeting shall make the required selection.

3. The election shall be by ballot.

SUPERINTENDENTS.

1. THEY shall be persons of decidedly religious principles, and appointed at the annual Teachers' Meeting.

2. They shall open and conclude the School by singing and prayer, they shall admit new Scholars and appoint them to their various Classes, arrange the Classes, maintain order, and direct and assist the Teachers, and see that the Scholars attend regularly and punctually the public worship of Almighty God.

3. The Superintendents shall be required to be at School 5 minutes before the time appointed for the Scholars, and it is expected they continue the whole of the time in the School, and with the Scholars in the Chapel.

TEACHERS.

1. EVERY Teacher shall be of unexceptionable moral character, and shall strictly conform to the rules of the School, be regular and punctual in attendance, and in case of unavoidable absence shall provide a proper substitute.

2. Any Person desirous of engaging as a Teacher shall signify his intention to the Superintendents, and if considered as proper he shall be admitted.

3. Each Teacher is expected to be at the School precisely at the time appointed. On entering he shall immediately repair to his place, and must avoid neglecting his duties as a Teacher either by leaving his class, or conversing with any person during School Hours, and at the time appointed shall conduct them to the House of God, and preserve decorum and attention during Divine Service. He shall see that his Scholars all kneel during the time of Prayer.

4. He shall call over the names of his Scholars after the opening service in the morning and afternoon, and in case of the absence of a Scholar for a whole day, shall be expected to ascertain the cause by a personal visit to the parents of the child.

5. Each Teacher shall be responsible for the good order and proper instruction of his Class, and shall endeavour to attain and practice the best modes of instruction, encouraging the diligent and admonishing those whose conduct is improper, and shall recommend such to higher classes whose carefulness and improvement merit advancement.

6. In all instructions given the Teachers are required to impress upon the minds of the Scholars the principles of religion, and by example and precept do all they can to solemnize the minds of the children.

7. A Catechism shall be provided for the senior Scholars, containing the fundamental doctrines of the Christian Religion; such as the being and providence of God; the total depravity of human nature; the atonement made by Christ for the sins of the whole world; the necessity of faith in that atonement to Salvation; and of the Spirit's influence to the formation of the Christian Character, and the Eternity of Rewards and Punishments.

8. No Teacher shall be allowed to inflict corporal punishment on the Children, but in cases of obstinacy or immorality shall refer the matter to the Superintendents.

9. Every Teacher must pay especial attention to the ringing of the bell, which shall be the signal at all times for the entire suspension of all work in which the School is engaged.

10. Any Teacher finding it necessary to discontinue his services, is requested to inform the Superintendents at the least a fortnight previous to his leaving, that another may be appointed in his place.

11. Teachers are earnestly desired to see that the books are used with care, and properly placed in the boxes, and shall on no account allow any to be taken from the School.

SCHOLARS.

1. CHILDREN of all denominations shall have free admission into this School, except such as have any infectious disorder, or having been discharged from the School are unable to give a satisfactory reason for their readmission, or whose parents will not be responsible for their regular attendance.

2. No child shall be admitted under 5 years of age, nor unless attended by one of its parents or friends duly authorised, or a note from them, requesting admission for such a child.

3. The times of attendance are from 9 till 12 in the Morning, and from a quarter to 3 till 4 in the Afternoon. Every Scholar is required to be punctual in his attendance, and to come to School neat and clean in person.

4. No Scholar (or Teacher) shall be allowed to bring any child that requires nursing, nor any fruit, or sweetmeats to eat in the School.

5. Any Scholar being in the habit of coming late to School will not be permitted to continue therein, and in case of absence from School 3 successive Sundays without a sufficient reason being given, shall be liable to be excluded.

6. If after repeated reproof, any Scholar be convicted of cursing, swearing, gaming, quarrelling, lying, using indecent language, &c., such shall forthwith be excluded.

7. No child can be removed from one class to another without the consent of the Superintendents.

J. TASKER, PRINTER, BOOKSELLER AND STATIONER, SKIPTON.

The 1850 rules of the Wesleyan Sunday School.

ABOVE: The working ladies and lads of Broughton Road Shed and
BELOW: a more genteel gathering.

Yesterday's people — some Skipton 'cartes visites' as the century turned.
(CDC)

Family footnote: ABOVE: the author's great Aunt Maggie — Margaret Mason — and her daughter at her cottage and shop, West Lane House, Embsay; Aunt Maggie lived to 98; BELOW: of Aunt Maggie's four sons, three were drowned in separate incidents — Roland survived.

Index

Figures in *italics* refer to illustrations

Subscribers
Presentation Copies

1 Skipton Town Council
2 Craven District Council
3 North Yorkshire County Council
4 Hepper Watson
5 Dacre Son and Hartley
6 Craven Museum
7 Cllr Bernard O'Neill
8 Cllr Norman Simpson

9 Geoffrey and Valentine Rowley
10 Kenneth Ellwood
11 Clive & Carolyn Birch
12 Wilfred Fattorini
13 The Lord of The Honour of Skipton
14 Hugh Fattorini
15 Mrs F. Wright
16 Linton Austen
17 Mr & Mrs A. Austen
18 A.J. Boxall
19 Robert William Parish
20 Stuart Gledhill
21 Mrs E. Wisbey
22 M.T. Quinn
23 Mrs Norah Dodd
24 H.N. Hartley
25 W.R.C. Houston JP FRICS
26 Miss M.E. Mason
27 David J. McConnell
28
29 D.C. Grant
30 Ermysted's Grammar School
31 Mrs J. Jessop
32 Colin Speakman
33 Jean Grainger
34 G. Throup
35 Mrs B. Mason
36 Peter Chard
37 David Aynesworth
38 P.J. Campbell
39 Victoria & Albert Museum
40 Mrs Wiseman
41 Major Roy Kilner MCTD
42 F.J. Hanson
43 Mrs D. Deakin
44 Mrs Joan Emmot
45 Mrs J. Ayrton
46 B.H. Wilkinson
47 Mr Brazier
48 K. Stephenson
49 R.G. Hall
50 The Librarian, Craven College

51 P.J. Crangle
52 Mrs Edna Wade
53 Mrs P. Midgley
54 Mrs I.R. Turner
55 Miss M. Ellis
56 B. Pate
57 Dr & Mrs A.D. Bundock
58 Stanley Brumfitt
59 Mrs Derek Suddards
60 Mrs M.E. Taylor
61 D.J. Bundock
62 E. Jackson
63 J.W. Monkhouse
64 Mrs C. Montgomery
65 K. Massheder
66 J.B. Price
67 J. Moorby
68 W.J. Hebden
69 Mrs Brenda Kirkbride
70 Mrs Broadbent
71 M. Broadbent
72 John Richardson
73 John Wright
74 Mrs F. Raw
75 Mrs M. Gardner
76 Mrs J. Crossley
77 Mrs R. Wilkinson
78 Keith Henderson
79 Sheila Coe
80 A. Barnes
81 Miss E. Clark
82 Mrs A. Banks
83
84 A. Gill
85 Mrs R. Barrett
86 Mrs J. Roberts
87 J.C. White
88 G. Glew
89 Mrs A. Walls
90 Mrs D. Makin
91 Mrs J.C. Pickles
92 Norman Cox
93 L. Barker
94 W. Bean
95 B.E. Nelson
96 B. Matthews
97 G.A. Strafford
98 D.W. Smith

99 Ermysteds' Grammar School Library
100 Mr & Mrs P.G. Hepworth
101 T. Moorby
102 E. Pettinger
103 Mrs J. Bundock
104 Dr C.D. Watkinson
105 R.E. Kirkbright
106 Mrs D. Hamshaw
107 Mrs B.M. Boxall
108 Dr & Mrs A.G. Cumberland
109 J.B. Padgett
110 Timothy Watkinson
111 N.D. Simpson
112 R.M. Styles
113 J.M. Linsley
114 G.H. Hunt
115 Mrs S. Bewes
116 Mrs E.C. Metcalfe
117 Mrs E. Barritt
118 G.H. Lofthouse
119 Mrs D. Taylor
120
121 J.R. Wilman
122 Mrs S.M. Garry
123 A.J. Broadley
124 Barbara Yerkess
125 George Staniforth
126 C.A. Smith
127
131 Dr J.F. Goodall
132 C.A. Smith
133 D. Wilkinson
134 Brian Walker
135 Jacqueline Ann Barrett
136 Thomas Redvers Bates
137 Nicola Helen Fox
138 Michael A. Holgate
139
140 Mrs R. Procter
141 Kenneth Lofthouse
142 Michael Walmsley
143
144 Mrs Carmen Fryers
145 James T. Crisp
146 Andrea Smith
147 Mrs D. Gill

148 Olive M. Hodgson
149 G.E.M. Widdop
150 J. Stuart
151 A. Pickles
152 David Naish
153 Katherine Farey
154 Megan G. Fluck
155 Craven Books
156 Bernard O'Neill
157 Ian Dewhirst
158 Skipton Business & Professional Women
166
167
168 J.K. Ellwood
169 Arthur Bilsborough
170 Mrs V. McGonigle
171 Mrs Enid I. Cheetham
172 Gurth Robinson
173 Joseph O'Neill
174 C.L. Boothman
175 Thomas Drake
176 Lawrence Gibbon
177 P.S. Longbottom
178 Mrs S. M. Brown
179 Mr & Mrs S.M.D. Brown
180 Mr & Mrs J.D.F. Brown
181 Mr & Mrs K. Lasky
182 Mr & Mrs J. Hill
183
184 C.W. Holden
185 H.R. Tempest
186
187 Mrs K. Claire Brooks
188
189 Harold S. Green
190 Wales, Wales &
191 Rawson
192 David A. Butcher
193 T. Wilson Goad
194 David Hill
195 Lionel Houghton
196 Sidney A.V. Irwin
197 J.H. Kinley
198 Mrs P. Robinson
199 Barrie W. Jones
200 Mrs G. Walters
201 Gerald Hurst Walker

202 Roger Mason	253 Joseph Harrison	305 Edwin Townson	355 Richard Hartley
203 Frank J. Moulden	254 A.H. Town	306 Waterfall Travel	356 Roger Ian Beck
204 D.E. Riddiough	255 Miss Marion Longthorn	307 F.B.A. Irving	357 T. Wear
205 J.M. Sheard		308 Megan G. Fluck	358 T.I. Roberts
206 Robert Smith	256 Mrs Joan Mackie	309 Katherine Farey	359 Mrs M. Roberts
207 Mrs Kathleen Russell	257	310 J.E. Heelis	360 James A. Robson
208 H.G. Parkinson	258 Mrs M.J.R. Bannister	311 Sidney Waterfall	361 W.H. Webster
209 Kenneth George Stapleton	259 Peter D. Green	312 Miss Janet Cockshott	362 Michael George Gill
	260 F.M. Clayton	313	363 Mrs E.P. Coughlan
210 Robert Smith	261 Alex W. Wade	314 Mr & Mrs H.M. Gill	364 T. Alker
211 R.J. Titterington	262 P.S. Baldwin	315 John R.D. Pollard	365 John Moorhouse
212 Wilfrid C. Wright	263 Mary Slayden	316 G. Hawkins	366 Helen Elkington
213 Ronald Mattock	264 Sir John Horsfall	317 Susan D. Brooks	367 H.D. Dixon
214 A.H. Norton	265 Mrs M.J. Foster	318 Kenneth Hudson	368 Philip N. Hargreaves
215 Frederick Manby	266 Keith L. Schofield	319 T.B. Pickford	369 T.R. Thwaite
216 J.R. Shepherd	267 Mrs Ruth Spencer	320 James Ronald Parker	370 Mrs Rita Berry
217 Ernest H. Hoyle	268 Brian Davies	321 Mrs James Masefield	371 Joyce Hartley
218 Kenneth Alan Knowles	269 Dr Enid M. Pyrah	322 Mrs E. Fisher	372 M. Adele Oliver
219 R.H. Hargreaves	270 W.A.F. McAdam	323 Joan Astbury	373 Margaret Taylor
220 221 Richard Randall	271 Arthur D. Taylor	324 Charles E. Bray	374 Mrs I.L. Hicks
	272 Marion H. Butchart	325 Mrs Dorothy Maunders	375 Alice Robinson
222 Eric Kirby	273 David S. Benjamin	326 Norman Williams	376 Mr. & Mrs. A. G. Cumberland
223 225 Bernard Riley	274 Vera Hanley	327 John Michael Dickinson	
	275 R.L. Brayshaw	328 Roy Willcock	377 Dr Anthony R. Rowley
226 J.A. Jeanes	276 Eric Wiggan	329 D. Summersgill	378 Richard V. Rowley
227 228 Mary S. Eastwood	277 Owen & Marion Brown	330 W.R. Abbott	379 Miss Pamela M. Rowley
	278 Joan & Peter Hollows	331 E.V. Tosney	380 J. Fawcett
229 Mrs Lucy Betts	279 H.G. Bottomley	332 C. Pickles	381 Mrs Edna Throup
230 Norman Leach	280 Julie C. Coyle	333 Timothy R. Smith	382 Christopher Victor Moug
231 Vincent Paget Smith	281 Dr A.G. Morgan	334 Dr David Martyn Morgan	
232 Jean Ewbank	282 J.N. Smallwood		383 Stephen R. Doughty
233 C.R. Worthy	283 W.J. Preston	335 R.P. Sheldon	384 E. Lodge
234 Edgar Leach MBE TD	284 D. Atkinson	336 L. Viles	385 B.P. Luxton
235 George Leatt	285 J.H. Capstick	337 Miss N. Driver	386 Thomas B. Chapman
236 John Gunby	286 C.J. Varley	338 Fred Parker	387 Edith I. Thornton
237 Philip John Rycroft	287 J.P.M. Moody	339 Chas W. Preston	388 I. Crompton
238 Harry G. Fell	288 Reginald Newiss	340 Paul Duke	389 Geoffrey Waller
239 Dr Peter Leach	289 E.J. Spencer	341 N. Preston	390 A. Rhodes
240 Roger W. Suddards	290 John Chaston	342 D. Preece	391 R.L. Smith
241 Mrs Ida Raw	291 294 Rothwell Bishop	343 Patricia D. Downing	392 Patricia Anne Hardy
242 243 E.J. Ewan		344 N.H. Bolton	393 Mrs E.M. Holgate
	295 Joan Dixon	345 F. Hardcastle	394 Mrs P. Guy
244 Betty Sissons	296 W.M. Mason	346 E.L. Needham	395 Carol Johnson
245 Stanley Nutter	297 William Foster	347 Warwick M. Stephens	396 Lilian Rycroft
246 Evelyn Smith	298 E.D. Wallbank	348 Patricia Harris	397 Joan Carroll
247 T. Clarke	299 Mrs M. Bamford	349 Albert Edward Wright	398 H.R.W. Atkinson
248 Mrs T. Clarke	300 Alec Wood	350 351 Maureen A. Pearce	399 H. Driver
249 William Mattock Mason	301 302 J.L. Feather		400 Colin Williamson
		352 R.G. Burke	
250 Edward Arthur Mason	303 Aireville Secondary	353 Gladys Watson	
251 Cyril Clarke	304 School	354 Glyn Foxton Fairhurst	
252 George D. Brown			

Remaining names unlisted

Key to Caption Credits

AHAG Abbey Hall and Art Gallery Kendal
EB   Mrs E. Bannister
MD   Miss M. Dean
SCL   Skipton Castle Limited
STC   Skipton Town Council

DW   David Williams
CDC   Craven District Council
DH   David Hyde Photography
JW   Joe Wiseman

ENDPAPERS: FRONT: John Wood's 1832 Plan of Skipton; BACK:
Springs Canal, Skipton. (Drawing by John T. Walker, 1914)